MW00328919

Praise for *Well Lived*

A life well lived, indeed. And a book well written. There are powerful, vivid stories here, and compelling and enduring lessons about life that Marty shared. Marty's life was truly remarkable and the highlight reel is long and rich. The number of people he has impacted seems too many to count. I do hope this book finds a large audience. These are important lessons, particularly in these challenging times.

—Adam Bryant
Author, *The Corner Office*
Former Reporter, Editor, and Columnist, *The New York Times*

Come gather round and listen to a master storyteller at work. With wit and warmth, Marty Holleran weaves tales of a life well lived with modest lessons about business, love, courage, and family. His stories will leave you laughing (a lot), teary (more than occasionally), but always admiring the generous, loving spirit of—in one of his own highest compliments—a helluva guy.

—Rick Smith
Former Editor-in-Chief, Chairman, and CEO, *Newsweek*

What greater legacy could anyone hope to leave behind than a life that was truly well lived? This book chronicles the journey through a man's life that everyone can strive to emulate and learn from.

As a young executive at GE, I was fortunate enough to be located at one of the stops on Marty's journey where, like many others, I was mentored and nurtured by this exceptional person. Most importantly, Marty took me under his wing and shared his valuable time. Through successes and failures, those lessons have endured and continued to serve as a beacon in both my life and business career.

From his humble beginnings in Scranton, PA, to the global boardrooms of corporate power, and the major challenges of everyday life we all face, this book takes us through the challenging and heartwarming life story of a very special man.

I urge everyone to join Marty on this fascinating trip and witness, page by page, what a life well lived is all about!

—Larry Johnston
Former Chairman and CEO, Alberston's Inc.

A great inspirational story! Marty has sure led a full life. A real live, rags-to-riches success story. Empathy, sincerity, family values, and old-fashioned Irish doggedness prevail. I have never known anybody as willful positive as Marty. This book is for anyone who likes a good human interest story and cherishes traditional American values. Younger people starting off in their careers will see what's possible to achieve and older people will identify with Marty in their own careers. I want my grandchildren to read this to absorb Marty's experience and see what's possible if you get your values straight and work hard.

—Sam Hoskinson
Former Vice Chairman, National Intelligence Council

On the surface of this book, you will read words about the life of a successful business executive and how it came to be. But this is less of a business book and more of a love story. It is a story of the true love between mother and son and how that love was multiplied many times over for the betterment of so many. Within the spectrum of true love exist two extremes: tears and smiles. Beneath the surface of these pages, the reader will experience much of both. This is a must read for high school and university graduates, those about to be married and expectant parents, and anyone who is willing to shed a tear and likes to chuckle.

—Brian O'Malley
President and CEO, Domino Foods, Inc.

WELL LIVED

MARTY HOLLERAN

Published by Advantage, Charleston, South Carolina.
Member of Advantage Media Group.

ADVANTAGE is a registered trademark, and the Advantage colophon is a trademark of Advantage Media Group, Inc.

Printed in the United States of America.

10 9 8 7 6 5 4 3 2 1

ISBN: 978-1-59932-930-7
LCCN: 2018947884

Cover design by George Stevens.
Layout design by Megan Elger.

This publication is designed to provide accurate and authoritative information in regard to the subject matter covered. It is sold with the understanding that the publisher is not engaged in rendering legal, accounting, or other professional services. If legal advice or other expert assistance is required, the services of a competent professional person should be sought.

Advantage Media Group is proud to be a part of the Tree Neutral® program. Tree Neutral offsets the number of trees consumed in the production and printing of this book by taking proactive steps such as planting trees in direct proportion to the number of trees used to print books. To learn more about Tree Neutral, please visit **www.treeneutral.com**.

Advantage Media Group is a publisher of business, self-improvement, and professional development books and online learning. We help entrepreneurs, business leaders, and professionals share their Stories, Passion, and Knowledge to help others Learn & Grow. Do you have a manuscript or book idea that you would like us to consider for publishing? Please visit **advantagefamily.com** or call **1.866.775.1696**.

This book is dedicated to my sons, Marty and Brian, who will carry on my name; to my daughter, Aileen, who will carry on my love; and to Kathy, my wonderful one, who is a wife, mother, and grandmother to our seven wonderful grandchildren.

Table of Contents

Acknowledgments

I would like to acknowledge the inputs from my wife, Kathy, my brothers, Charles and Jim; my children, Marty, Aileen, and Brian; my son-in-law, John Crowley; and my dear friend, Larry Johnston. I would like to thank Gary Strack and Rich Cooper for all of their input on the marketing of my book. A special acknowledgement goes to the staff at Advantage|ForbesBooks for all of their help. Last, but certainly not least, I'd like to acknowledge Eyre Price for his professional guidance in helping me craft the flow of the words in my story.

Forewords

Marty Holleran is my big brother.

To me, this would seem the only identifier he would need in his life.
But, no.

So, when he voiced an interest in writing a book about his life, I was frank and forthright in my opinion that I thought it was a terrible idea.

A really awful idea.

One of his worst—and trust me, that's saying something.

Still, I feel like I should explain these reservations.

It wasn't that I didn't think he *could* write a book—my big brother can do (almost) anything he puts his mind to. He's Irish, after all, and stubborn as a mule that way.

My concerns were more along the lines that I didn't think he should. Or, to be more exact, I didn't want him to feel like he *needed* to write a book.

Books like that are supposed to be written by ex-presidents and celebrities, newsmakers and people who promise to make their readers gazillionaires. That's all fine.

There are, however, far too many books written by folks who have very little to say. I think that's because the authors must feel some need for confirmation or adoration.

I know my big brother, I've seen the life he's built for himself, and it troubled me to think that with all of the riches in his world, he still might feel that same empty compulsion.

Then I read this book.

And I understood.

What you're holding in your hands isn't really a memoir, although you will certainly learn quite a bit about my big brother. (And a few things about me that are recounted much differently than I remember them!)

It's not a business book, although in these pages are all the secrets to the fabulous career my brother has built for himself, and I'm certain his words of wisdom would prove valuable to anyone wishing to improve their professional situation.

What this book is—what it *really* is—is the rarest of things.

A love letter.

A real, honest-to-God, from-the-heart love letter.

To his beautiful wife, Kathy.

To his kids. And grandkids. Nephews and nieces.

To me (his favorite!) and our brothers and our mother and father.

To all those people who shared his dream of making a business "dance" and played their part on one of the many teams he's organized over the course of his career.

This is a love letter to his life.

I am glad that he wrote it.

I am glad that I read it.

And in two hundred pages, you will be, too.

—**CHARLES HOLLERAN**

Being the oldest child carries with it a host of familial responsibilities. And don't even get me started on all of the nonsense that my younger sister, Aileen, and brother, Brian, got away with that never would've been tolerated from me, the first.

Yet being the oldest has also offered me a host of opportunities.

The greatest of these has been carrying the name Marty Holleran.

My father's name.

My hero's name.

Now, I realize many boys come to regard their father in that way, but few have more justification for doing so.

While others in his position might have turned themselves over to their careers and their own interests, my dad always made it clear to me and my mother and siblings—not in his words, but in his actions—that we were his priority. In all the ball games and school plays, the homework help and fatherly advice. In what he gave to us *and* what he refused us.

In the end, a life is really no more than a matter of time—that's the only thing of any real value that we have.

My father always made sure to give us all that we needed.

It's because of this that I am the man I am today.

And that my sister and brother are who they are.

And for all that he shared with us, I'm glad and grateful that he's now shared some measure of that same special gift with the world within the pages of this book.

It's just another reason I'm proud to bear the name I do.

—**MARTY HOLLERAN III**

Some years ago, I was honored to be recognized as a recipient of the Torch of Freedom award by the Anti-Defamation League.

The occasion was particularly meaningful for me because just a few years earlier, I had sat in that very room among the audience as I watched my mentor, Marty Holleran, receive the same honor.

There on the dais, it seemed to me like a full circle of sorts. Or, rather, like walking the path that Marty had shown to me had led us both to that same podium.

So when it was my turn, I made certain to thank a handful of people, but at the top of my list was my great friend and mentor, Marty Holleran.

I have been very fortunate in business. As a result, I'm frequently asked for my "secrets" to success and maximizing one's career.

There are, of course, no substitutes for hard work and perseverance.

Brains don't hurt, either.

But all of that—and whatever other special skills you may bring to the table—I can think of nothing more valuable to a junior person making their first serious forays into the business world (or any endeavor, really) than the active participation and guidance of a mentor.

While I was at GE (and continuing to this day), Marty took me under his wing and was generous in sharing his time, knowledge, and experience. He gave me the opportunity to realize success and trusted me to recover from my failures—and I learned much from both situations.

I cannot make promises regarding results. I can simply tell you that following the examples and lessons that Marty Holleran provided to me was one of the most important contributions to my career. Those same lessons are set out here in this book—in Marty's own inimitable way—and I am confident that everyone would benefit from incorporating them into professional and personal approaches.

—LARRY JOHNSTON

I'm keenly aware that it is truly a special thing for a young man to have someone to shepherd him through the trials and tribulations of life. And in a way, I have been blessed to have two special men play this impactful role in my life.

When I first met Marty Holleran, he was the father of a young woman I was dating. Still, there was never a moment of the uncomfortable tension that so often characterizes those awkward introductions. Instead, he welcomed me into his wonderful family with open arms from the very beginning.

When I married the love of my life, his daughter Aileen, there was no hesitation to turn his daughter over to my care. Instead, Marty made clear that he trusted me completely with one of the most precious people in his life—and that if there was ever a time of need, we were both under his care.

When those dark times arrived—true to his unspoken word—he offered me everything I needed and more. And when the skies cleared, he never mentioned any of it again, which in my book is as much a testament to his character as the mountains he moved for me and my family. Friend. Mentor. Protector. Marty Holleran is now and always will be, simply—Dad.

—JOHN CROWLEY

Irish men. They're always trying to get the last word on one another, when they should know that's impossible when there's an Irish woman in the mix.

Just like they should know that every man's strengths and weaknesses are made greater or lesser by the woman at his side.

Marty Holleran's life has indeed been "well lived," and I have been no small part of all that.

Three wonderful children.

Seven angelic grandchildren.

Twelve houses in the first twenty years—and I'd no sooner get one just the way I wanted it when Marty would walk through the door with a bottle of champagne in his hand and a sheepish grin on his face. "I have news …"

Champagne. God, how I learned to hate the stuff (just kidding).

But, God, how I love that man.

People ask me if I believe in love at first sight, and I always respond that it's not a matter of belief for me. I know it happens. It may be rarer than rare for the rest of the world, but I knew the first time I set eyes on Marty Holleran that I'd found the love of my life.

And as Marty will tell you, I am always right.

Marty and I have gone through this life hand in hand. Good times and not-so-good times. But always hand in hand.

And even now after all these years, I have to tell you that I melt just a little each and every time I look into his eyes and see the way he looks at me.

And so I know I've been lucky to have him, too.

That's why I am beyond pleased to have the honor of the last word and to introduce all of you to the remarkable story of the most remarkable man I know, and love with all my heart—Marty Holleran.

—KATHY HOLLERAN

Introduction

When I first considered writing a memoir, I was uncertain of the soundness of such an undertaking and floated the idea by someone whose judgment I've always trusted and relied on.

They were not a fan of the idea.

Not at all.

In fact, I think the phrase "I implore you not to ..." appeared once or twice in their well-intended response.

There were several reasons for that reaction, but primarily their reservations boiled down to a single concern: "You're not rich and famous, and therefore you can't tell anyone else how to become rich and famous."

And that is absolutely true.

I have had the good fortune to enjoy a long and rewarding career that has allowed me to become both very comfortable in my lifestyle and well regarded within my professional community.

But I am not "rock star" rich and certainly I'm no household name or tabloid fodder.

What I am, however, is enormously grateful and fundamentally happy.

And in these times, which seem to be marked by a general societal discontent fueled by a pervasive sense of entitlement to instant gratification and a gnawing, unquenchable desire for more and more and more ... well, grateful and happy seem like the rarer and more desirable of conditions.

The book you're holding now is evidence that, after careful consideration, I chose to continue on with writing my memoir. That doesn't mean that I simply disregarded that piece of advice, because I treasure their counsel and continue to seek it out in all aspects of my life.

And it certainly doesn't mean that I think those observations were wrong.

To the contrary, my ultimate decision to write this book was fueled by the fact that those opinions were absolutely dead on the money. If what you're after is fortune and fame, I know very little about how to get you started down that road.

Instead, my intention (and sincere hope) is that by sharing some of the formative events of my personal life and successes in my business career, I might be able to entertain you and—maybe, just maybe—provide you with the blueprints I've followed to make my life such an enormously rewarding experience, filled with love and friendship and purpose. Maybe in these

Maybe in these pages, you'll find some inspiration for writing your own life story, some instruction on how to blend together your professional goals and personal ambitions, and some guidance on how to find the balance between making a living and living a life.

pages, you'll find some inspiration for writing your own life story, some instruction on how to blend together your professional goals and personal ambitions, and some guidance on how to find the balance between making a living and living a life.

To that end, I hope my story leaves you all just as happy as I've been in writing it.

That's all.

And that was reason enough for me to write down what follows.

In the end, all I can wish for is that when you've turned the last page I have made you laugh, maybe caused you to shed a tear or two, and that I've given you some inspiration to live a life that, if not filled with riches and fame, is a little bit like mine ... well lived.

Chapter One

THE LONG AND (NOT SO) LONELY NIGHT

Life is filled with painful little ironies.

On that particular evening, the razor-edged irony stabbing me right in the heart was that I was alone.

As long as I can remember, I have always been "the guy," the one who was always there for others. When I was young, it was the kids in school or the little boy down the block. After tragedy struck, it was my brothers and father. As a grown man, it was the junior executives who served under me and—more often than anyone might've expected—the more senior ones, too.

Even now, I find that the greatest satisfaction I've ever realized in my professional career comes to me in my current role as a private corporate mentor, fostering some of America's top executive talent.

I have made a life out of being there for others, but on that particular night I was alone.

Completely alone.

The year was 1991. The era of mergers, acquisitions, hostile takeovers. George H.W. Bush was president, and business school grads in tailored suits and power ties ruled the world and made obscene amounts of money buying up whole companies and then selling them off piece by piece.

And those were just the kids.

For someone with my extensive corporate experience, there were more than a few opportunities that would have tempted any executive, and when one particularly tantalizing prospect came my way, I suppose I thought, "Why not me?"

And at the time, I couldn't find a single reason.

There certainly wasn't any competing professional responsibility preventing me.

I'd happily and faithfully spent the majority of my career with American icon General Electric, but at that particular time, the long and winding road of my career path had led me to a post as president and chief executive officer of Thomson Consumer Electronics, Marketing and Sales Company, a French national company that had acquired General Electric's consumer electronics business. In the years following, the French national corporation instituted France's unique corporate culture throughout the business, and that meant there was a greater focus on doing things the "French way," even at the cost of the overall bottom line, and an even greater resistance to anything American—and I was about as American as you could get.

Personal chemistry is one of the most important components in any business relationship, and

Personal chemistry is one of the most important components in any business relationship.

I knew that the complete lack of any connection with the Franco-phile who chaired the board meant that it was only a matter of time before I'd be saying "Adieu."

So when a group of financiers came along with a proposition they wanted to talk over with me, I listened.

It was a simple pitch.

They had put together a group that wanted to take over a NYSE-traded electronics company. It doesn't matter now who they were, but they were big enough that everyone in my world knew them well, and they were such significant players that I immediately took interest in what they had to say.

They had the necessary financing in place, and the business plan they presented to me seemed rock solid.

I liked what I heard—liked it a lot.

Even in the era of Wild West Wall Street, this was one of those you-worked-all-your-life-for-this opportunities.

Really, once-in-a-lifetime stuff.

The offer first put on the table was chief operating officer, but the prospect of chief executive officer was dangled in front of me as more of a promise than a possibility. There was a terrific package—all of the perks and benefits and incentives you could've reasonably demanded, and more than a few extras I never would have thought to ask for.

Anyone would've jumped at the chance.

Or at least I did.

And things started off well enough.

Of course, that's the way things like that always start off.

But the certainty I'd had going into the situation only height-ened the surreal effect I felt swirling around me a short time later, on that long, lonely evening when I found myself in my well-appointed office, seated at my designer desk with my letter of resignation in front of me.

As I said, it all started well enough. I had the corner office with all the accoutrement and a team of really top people surrounding and supporting me.

We were all focused on the challenge of taking this well-known but time-worn enterprise into a new era, and the entire business was supposed to be mine to rebuild from the foundations on up, to shape in my corporate philosophy—and my philosophy was "Let's make this business dance!"

> **The entire business was supposed to be mine to rebuild from the foundations on up, to shape in my corporate philosophy— and my philosophy was "Let's make this business dance!"**

It was thrilling in that way that only a new experience can be. Although I'd been in the corporate world for over four decades, this was my first experience in being fully immersed in a project from the financing on up, and I relished each progressive step as another opportunity to learn some new skill set. And while I might not have always been the quickest learner in the classroom, I have always been the hardest working guy in the room. Any room.

I talked to bankers and learned their language. I came to view business from an entirely new perspective. I rolled up my sleeves and worked my way through the books. All of them.

In fact, I learned more about running a public company in that first year than I could have ever imagined. I dug right down into the details.

Of course, we all know what lurks there in the details.

And, sure enough, the devil was hiding in there among all those columns of numbers.

At first, there were just … let's call them *concerns*. That's all. Concerns.

But over time, those concerns intensified and worsened until they were too significant to ignore any longer—or at least I couldn't turn away from them any longer.

Don't get me wrong—there were no actual improprieties that I was aware of, not in any legal sense. Still, it became increasingly obvious to me that the CEO, the man orchestrating the takeover and pulling strings behind the scenes—including my hire—had no genuine aspirations for bettering the company's fortunes and restoring it to the dominant market position it had once held. Instead, those devilish details made clear that the plan from the very beginning had been to drive the company into bankruptcy and then buy back the more favorable pieces at a significant savings—and profit.

There was nothing illegal with the plan. As I said, it was 1991. This was all just another day at work across much of America and the world.

But that didn't mean it sat well with me.

And that's why I sat there with my letter of resignation.

Since I was a little boy, I have had what I refer to as my "moral compass." It is my personal conscience, not governed by laws or regulations, not influenced by times or fashion. It is an absolute ethical North Star that has always guided me, even through the darkest of nights.

Even through long, lonely nights like that one.

Now, when I say I was completely alone, I mean just that.

Not only was there no one there to talk to, no sage to back-and-forth with over my dilemma and offer me some badly needed advice, but all the support personnel had left for the evening and there wasn't even someone to take care of that last clerical matter of sending off my defiant resignation letter. And that meant I had to walk my letter all the way down the hall to the fax machine.

I have a master's degree in electrical engineering and had been working with complicated electronics for my entire adult life. I had just proven I was capable of engineering a multimillion dollar takeover, but I confess that the candy-colored buttons on that fax machine confused me for a moment.

I stood and looked down at my letter in the tray waiting to be sent.

Second thoughts multiplied.

I questioned whether I might be overreacting, wondered whether it might be best to simply go along with the plan. My three kids were all grown and thriving on their own, but it was still a monumental step for me to walk away from a position of that stature and significance.

And I have to admit that I definitely considered whether the sensible thing might be to surrender my moral compass—just this once—to collect the fortune that had been promised me and then get on with my life.

I have to admit that I definitely considered whether the sensible thing might be to surrender my moral compass—just this once—to collect the fortune that had been promised me and then get on with my life.

The fax machine seemed to be taunting me, waiting for me to make up my mind.

One push of the button and my letter would appear a fraction of a second later in the CEO's office in Switzerland and then that would be that. There would be no taking it back once it was sent. That would be that.

Alea iacta est.

That's Latin for "The die is cast."

The Roman historian Suetonius claimed that this stoic aside is all that Julius Caesar said as he crossed the Rubicon river, unequivocally declaring his intentions to challenge Pompey for Rome itself.

I thought about the Jesuits who had taught me this bit of historical trivia in college.

And I thought about the nuns and priests who had provided my educational foundation.

I wondered what they would tell me to do in this moment of personal crisis, with my career in the "send" tray and my finger on the button.

I thought about my brothers and what they might expect from me.

I thought about my children and what I would expect from them.

I thought about my mother and my father. My wife, Kathy.

I thought about everyone who had played such important roles in my life, who had contributed to my life in so many different ways, who had played some role in making me the man who was standing there before that unnecessarily complicated fax machine, ready to scuttle my once-in-a-lifetime opportunity for nothing more than the moral compass that had sustained me through my life.

I thought about each and every one of them.

Suddenly, I wasn't so alone anymore.

And my thoughts drifted back to the very beginning …

Chapter Two

OUR HOUSE

I was born in Scranton, Pennsylvania, in the 1940s.

If you ever heard Vice President Joe Biden talk with love about our shared hometown, then you already know everything about the environment that defined my formative years.

If, however, you're a stranger to my hometown, then let me introduce you now.

At the beginning of the twentieth century, Scranton was third only to Philadelphia and Pittsburgh in terms of size and significance in the state of Pennsylvania. It became known as the Electric City, but it was coal that had put it on the map, with veins of anthracite running all up and down the Lackawanna Valley. There were dozens of factories, too, and a bustling downtown that thrived in the early years of Eisenhower's post-war economy.

At this time, Scranton was still very much a city defined by its immigrant origins, and because of that the neighborhoods were unofficially, but very strictly, segregated according to national origins.

Bull's Head. Providence. Green Ridge. The Hill Section and Minooka. They were all Scranton, but each was its own ethnic enclave.

I was born in Scranton's South Side, which had a sprinkling of Italians and Polish, but overall the area could hardly have been more Irish if it had been packed up and dropped down on the Emerald Isle itself. Mailboxes had names like McAndrew, Vaughn, Burke, Bohan, Lavelle, Donovan, and Cawley.

Home was 1522 Prospect Avenue. Four bedrooms, one bath. A small house, I suppose—at least by today's standards—but back then it was more than enough room for the lot of us. And that makes me smile, because there were a lot of us in the lot of us: my mother and father; my three brothers, Jack, Charles, and Jim; my grandmother and grandfather, Charles and Jennie Biglin; three uncles, Ray, Gav and James Biglin; Aunt Kathryn; three cousins, Elaine, Paula and Jimmy Biglin; and occasional long visits from my cousin Jerome Flynn who later became my academic advisor when I went to college.

All of us under one roof.

And I know it's hard to believe—I can hardly believe it myself—but I cannot remember a single harsh word among the lot of us for the entire time we were there. No drama. No nastiness. There was none of the negativity that seems to have infected far too many homes these days.

I cannot remember a single harsh word among the lot of us for the entire time we were there.

My father, also named Marty, was a simple man, a salesman by trade, but I remember him best as the gentle leader of our clan. He was always patient and kind, even when the addition of this brother-in-law or that to our already cramped quarters might have understandably strained another man's composure from time to time.

He was always quick with a joke, and if you asked him how his day on the road had gone, his answer was more likely based on how many laughs he'd gotten than sales he'd made. He called getting a smile "cracking their face" and he would tell me stories of resistant customers who would meet him with a stony grimace, fixed on denying him the satisfaction of even a grin. Whether he made the sale or not, he was always determined to leave them with a smile.

And he always did.

My mother, Aileen, was a Marywood College graduate, which was extremely unusual for someone of her generation. I always knew her as a mom who stayed at home like almost every other woman of the day, but she had been a Latin teacher once.

Whether he made the sale or not, he was always determined to leave them with a smile.

One day I asked her why she didn't teach anymore.

At that moment, the door burst open and my little brother Jim came running into the house, whooping and hollering.

She smiled at the intrusion and told me simply, "*That's* why I don't teach anymore. One day I may go back to work, but right now you and your brothers are the best job I could ever have and I don't want to miss a moment of that."

To me they were just Mom and Dad.

But even before I had the maturity necessary for any sort of serious introspection or intellectual appreciation of their contributions to my life, I was always aware that they were the shining examples of what I most wanted to be when I grew up: good and decent people.

Chapter Three

MY MORAL COMPASS

In addition to my parents, the other important influence in my early life came from the Church, which played an integral part in our whole community and was like the head of a larger, interconnected family.

My weekdays were spent at the neighborhood parochial school under the tutelage of the parish priest and a collection of nuns. Saturdays were frequently dominated by confession, in preparation for Mass on Sunday. And Sunday, of course, was the Lord's Day, when I either served Mass as an altar boy or sang in the choir.

And so whether I was at home or out and about in a community presided over by the Church, there were always authority figures present to instill in me a strong ethical code and to build on that principled foundation.

As a result, there were no gray moral areas for me in those days. Things were right or wrong, good or bad. I willingly incorporated those values into my behavior and have always tried to live my life accordingly—even when it wasn't easy.

I remember the first time I learned the hard lesson of just how expensive that code of conduct could be.

When I was about ten or eleven, I became a paperboy. For me, it was a way to earn a little extra money to cover my tab for soda and ice cream at the Sunshine Shop, the neighborhood corner store. My parents, however, saw the position as a way of teaching me that there are rewards for a job well done beyond just receiving a paycheck.

Looking back now, I see that the job provided me with both.

I was a good paperboy, too. I delivered my customer's copies of the *Scranton Times* without fail, no matter the weather or whatever after-school activities my friends might have been up to.

I knew all the tricks of the trade: how to fold the paper, where to stand on the sidewalk and the proper flick of the wrist needed to send a tucked paper spiraling end over end through the air with just enough velocity to make it to the customer's porch, and, most important of all, not hitting anything but the porch.

I was a total pro.

There was a kid in our neighborhood who was younger than me by five years and seriously impressed by an older boy with a job of his own and a perfect arch to his paper toss. He used to follow me around on my route, and if I ever pretended back then that he was a pest or bother, I'll freely confess right now that I got a kick out of being his hero.

One afternoon, after observing my consistent right-on-the-porch tosses, he asked me if he could try throwing one. It seemed a simple request, coming as it did from my #1 fan.

I handed him a paper and gave him a quick tutorial on the mechanics of the proper toss.

He took aim at the porch, wound up just like I'd shown him, and then let it fly …

I knew immediately that something was very, very wrong, but it was one of those moments when time slows to a near stop just to give you an extra moment or two to appreciate the disaster that's about to occur. We stood there together, watching that paper turn end over end across the afternoon sky.

There was nothing I could do.

The paper hit the plate glass window at the front of the house dead square in the center, and it sounded like a bomb had gone off, followed very quickly by the tinkling of a thousand shards of glass.

> It was one of those moments when time slows to a near stop just to give you an extra moment or two to appreciate the disaster that's about to occur.

As I stood there flat-footed on the sidewalk, I realized I had three options: the first animal instinct was to run, but I dismissed that notion almost as quickly as it hit me.

The second option was to turn on my little friend and place all of the blame on his thin shoulders. And in fairness, he was the one who had actually thrown that errant paper.

I'm confident that more than a few boys of my age and in my shoes would have chosen to do just that, and I admit that I considered it for a second or two.

In the end, however, neither of those options worked for me. Instead, that moral compass of mine was pointing right up the stairs to the front door of that house—and that was where I marched.

There was no need to ring the doorbell—my customers were already out on the porch.

They were none too happy with what had been delivered that afternoon, and freely expressed their … let's call it consternation.

I never said a word in my defense nor explained that I hadn't been the one to throw the errant paper. Instead, I took responsibility for the entire situation. I was the paperboy, and it was my paper that had shattered the window, and the only words that came out of my mouth that day was a promise to pay for a new window.

In the end, the price of my moral compass: a whole week's wages.

That might just be the best money I ever spent in my childhood.

Chapter Four

SHIP OF DREAMS

Among the crowd of us living in that tiny house on Prospect Avenue—for a time, at least—was our Uncle Gav.

He was a great guy. A loving and supportive member of the family. And a fine uncle to all his nephews.

He was also one of the smartest men I've ever known, well educated with advanced degrees, at a time when those kinds of academic accomplishments were extremely rare.

Maybe it was the claustrophobic confines of our living space, or maybe it was the life events that had driven him there, but whatever the reason, one day Uncle Gav got it into his head that what he really wanted to do in this world was to put out onto open water in a boat of his own making.

Now, Scranton has a namesake lake, and Roaring

Uncle Gav got it into his head that what he really wanted to do in this world was to put out onto open water in a boat of his own making.

Brook converges with the Lackawanna River just a mile or so from our house. But for the most part there's a conspicuous shortage of navigable waters in the greater Scranton area.

None of this deterred Uncle Gav.

Of course, this great shipbuilding adventure started out as just another round of the "Wouldn't it be great if ..." conversations he and my father would engage in around the kitchen table for hours on end, but soon enough he had hand-drawn sketches and lists of supplies he'd need to tackle the job.

And then, much to everyone's surprise, there was noise and activity in our cellar.

Sawing and planing. Hammering and occasional cursing.

Uncle Gav was actually building a boat in our basement.

To my brothers and me, this was a tremendously exciting event. After all, there wasn't another boat being built anywhere in South Side.

Uncle Gav was actually building a boat in our basement.

I'm not sure what my mother and father made of it, but I think now that they must have just been glad that Uncle Gav was doing something.

Granted, a lot of what he was doing was sitting at the kitchen table talking about what he planned to do next or how exciting his days out on the water were going to be, but there were frequent blasts of actual activity down the cellar steps.

And this shouldn't in any way call his genius or skills into question. Just the opposite.

What he crafted day after day in our cellar was a beautiful vessel. Every line was carefully calculated and shaped; every plank of wood was expertly sanded and stained and sealed.

And then there arrived a day when Uncle Gav was finally finished and the only tasks that remained were to christen the boat and set her free upon the water with her builder/captain at the helm. It was a momentous event, and all of the Holleran men were summoned for the Herculean task of lifting and carrying the vessel up and out of the basement.

And therein lay the problem.

Uncle Gav had built the boat of his dreams, but it was too damn big and heavy to make it out of the basement. For all of the hundreds of calculations he'd made, he'd forgotten the one that was most necessary to actually get it to water.

I'll never forget the look on his face as he stood there pondering his blunder, a mixture of amused embarrassment and resigned heartbreak.

He made some more notes and scribbled down some equations, calculations he was confident would help him lick the problem, but Uncle Gav's boat never made it out of the cellar, never had that maiden voyage he'd spent so many hours dreaming about and working towards.

He talked about salvage efforts from time to time, but mainly just to offer his landlocked goof up to the rest of us for a good-natured laugh at his expense or to complain about what he saw as life's cruel intent to single him out for disappointment.

Mostly, however, he just forgot about his boat. And his dream.

When we were just boys, it was funny as hell to my brothers and me.

We all laughed and laughed.

As we got older, however, that boat in the basement came to represent something else.

Whenever one of us would be pondering one life step or another, the rest would goad him with the best of intentions. "Are you just sitting around the kitchen table, building Uncle Gav's boat, or are you *really* going to do something?"

Whenever one of us would be pondering one life step or another, the rest would goad him with the best of intentions. "Are you just sitting around the kitchen table, building Uncle Gav's boat, or are you *really* going to do something?"

When I look back, the story still makes me smile, but now I see the tragedy, too.

So much squandered time and wasted effort.

But worst of all ... those lost dreams, too precious and rare to have been surrendered so easily.

I sometimes wonder whether Uncle Gav ever had any real plans to put that boat in the water. I think if he had, he would've made the plans necessary to get it out of the basement. I suspect he never trusted his boat (or his dream) and sabotaged them both from the beginning.

My Uncle Gav. A fine man and a great uncle.

I'll hold him in my heart till I die, grateful that without really trying he taught me one of life's most important lessons: It doesn't matter how smart you are or what degrees you have. It doesn't matter how badly you want to achieve something. Or even how hard you work towards that goal. None of that matters if you don't have a workable plan to get from where you are to where you want to be.

You have to have a plan for getting your boat out of the basement.

Chapter Five

THREE KINDS OF TROUBLE

Because I'd assumed responsibility for that shattered window and made good on my promise to repair it, I didn't get in trouble for what happened. Not with my parents, and not with the Church or the *Scranton Times.*

Still, I was one of four boys, and so trouble wasn't necessarily foreign to me, either.

Back in those days, there were three tiers of trouble that a kid could find himself in.

One-name trouble. "Marty, you know better than that."

Two-name trouble. "Marty Holleran, I don't know what gets into you sometimes."

And then there was three-name trouble.

When I think of three-name trouble, I always think of one particular event, probably because they were not my three names that were invoked. Instead, it was my brother, Charlie, who was in the hot seat.

Or the confessional booth, as it happened to be.

It was a Saturday afternoon, and the Holleran boys were in line for our weekly confessions. Charlie's turn came, and he'd just closed the door behind him—the door that is supposed to keep a confessor's identity and sins a secret—when all of a sudden, everyone in a two-block radius heard the parish priest explode: "Charles. Benedict. Holleran."

Ten seconds later, my younger brother emerged, red faced and visibly shaken.

I was the first to get to him. "What in the world just happened?"

Conscious that everyone in the church was staring at him, he took me aside and whispered, "I told Father I had a girlfriend and confessed that I'd touched her in an impure way." (In those days, that probably meant he'd touched her bare shoulder. By accident.)

We were teenagers, so this didn't quite explain the priest's volcanic reaction.

"Is that all?"

Charlie grimaced. "Father asked me if she was in the family way and I said yes."

That explained the explosion.

It was funny, but I also knew it to be an impossibility at the time. "Why would you say she's in the family way?"

"Well, she is," Charlie insisted. "She lives with her mom and her dad, brothers and sisters. She lives with her whole family."

And that was the day that I learned that while it's very important to choose your words carefully, it's even more essential that you make sure that others understand what you mean.

Chapter Six

THE GIFT THAT KEEPS ON GIVING

While my family never had much in terms of material luxuries, I can't say that any of us felt that we were doing without, either. There was always a roof over our heads, a hot supper on the table, and clean clothes on our backs.

There was also money for a few extras.

One day when I was just a boy, my mother sat me on her lap. "I can't give you everything that I want to, but there are two things I'm going to make sure you get. The first is all of my love, and that's easy because it's free." She proved that with a hug.

"The second thing I'm going to give you is the gift of self-confidence."

My face must have betrayed my confusion.

She explained. "A man who can sing and dance will always have friends, and making friends, having people like you, that's the secret to life. Do that and everything else will take care of itself. So, I'm going to make sure you learn to sing and dance, because if you can handle the spotlight on a stage, then you can do the same when your turn comes in life's spotlight."

I'd be lying to say that I understood exactly what she was talking about, but I have learned since that day—ten thousand times over—that she was absolutely right. Hers was, without question, the single best piece of advice I ever received in my life.

And so I began singing lessons. Dance lessons. Any kind of lessons that she could get me to take. I sang pop songs and Irish ballads. I danced jazz and tap. Sometimes I sang and danced, both at the same time.

And I was good.

Very good. At least, as a singer.

> I sang all the time. And the more I did, the more comfortable I became in the spotlight—not only on a stage, but in life as well.

And soon singing became not only what I did, but what I wanted to do. I sang all the time. And the more I did, the more comfortable I became in the spotlight—not only on a stage, but in life as well.

Since then, there's not a day that goes by that I don't think of my mother and the gifts that she gave me. In this life, most people stand in the crowd and watch whatever happens to be on stage. Most people never get up there themselves, to feel all eyes on them and face the very real prospect of failing spectacularly. And that is how they live their lives.

> My mother put me on stage, where I bombed more than once, but where I learned to pick myself up and carry on anyway.

My mother put me on stage, where I bombed more than once, but where I learned to pick myself up and carry on anyway.

My mother wanted two things for me, and she was successful in bestowing both her gifts. I can still feel her warm embrace around me today. And every day of my life has been blessed and enhanced by the gift of self-confidence.

Chapter Seven

ON TOUR

When I say I was a good singer, that's not me bragging. It's just a fact.

My neighborhood had a theater, the Globe, and once a month they held an amateur night talent contest for entertainers across the city of Scranton. The prize was $35, a significant sum at the time.

I won the contest and walked away with that prize money in my pocket. Not once.

Or twice.

But every time. Winning became such a part of my routine that the $35 purse became a regular, budgeted source of income for me.

I was the Sinatra of Scranton's South Side.

And things only got better.

Among the many lessons that I took was a regular course in jazz at Jimmy Sutton's School of Dance. Jimmy was a real pro who'd made the rounds of the dance world, and I don't think I'm being unkind to say that he was generally unimpressed by pretty much everyone he encountered as a middle-aged dance teacher in Scranton.

And as a dancer, I'll admit that I wasn't anything better than fair. But when I sang for the man, I could tell right away that I'd done the seemingly impossible—I had impressed Jimmy Sutton.

A short time later, Jimmy took me aside and explained that he'd been asked to put together a youth group to go on tour as a USO show and he wanted me to be the soloist. The first stop: Lajes Field, Portugal in the Azores.

At that time, I'd never been out any farther than Atlantic City, and even that meager expedition had made me the Marco Polo of my neighborhood. Most of my friends (and their parents, too) had never ventured much beyond Scranton's city limits; maybe some adventurous few had made it as far as Wilkes-Barre to the south or Binghamton to the north.

So to be fourteen years old and find yourself as the star of a USO show on a military transport plane headed to an Army base in the Azores is … well, it was not unlike what someone might feel today if they were on a spaceship headed to Mars. It was that outrageous.

> **To be fourteen years old and find yourself as the star of a USO show on a military transport plane headed to an Army base in the Azores is … well, it was not unlike what someone might feel today if they were on a spaceship headed to Mars.**

I'd been singing in the family kitchen since I could speak and been a part of the church choir since I was in short pants. I had sung at school assemblies and on stage for prize money at the Globe, but getting out on a stage 2,636 miles from home, in front of an endless sea of servicemen, was more than I could have ever imagined.

And for one terrifying moment, more than I thought I was capable of.

The emcee came over the microphone. "Let's have a big welcome for our soloist, a fine young man from Scranton, Pennsylvania, Marty Holleran."

There was some polite applause and then an airfield packed with soldiers fell dead quiet.

In that terrifying moment of silence, it became apparent to me that maybe a large group of GIs on R&R confined to an island in the middle of the Atlantic didn't necessarily have listening to the song stylings of a teenaged crooner at the top of their what-to-do-for-fun list.

I stepped out to the front of the stage.

The only sound I could hear was my heart thumping in my chest.

All eyes were on me—exactly as my mother had promised.

I opened with "Danny Boy."

And then went into "How Ireland Got Its Name."

By the time I started my closer, "Dear Old Donegal," the audience was mine.

And I was theirs.

You're as welcome as the flowers in May to dear old Donegal. Meet Branigan, Fannigan, Milligan, Gilligan, Duffy, McCuffy, Malachy, Mahone, Rafferty, Lafferty, Donnelly, Connelly, Dooley, O'Hooley, Muldowney, Malone, Madigan, Cadigan, Lanihan, Flanihan, Fagan, O'Hagan, O'Hoolihan, Flynn, Shanihan, Manihan, Fogarty, Hogarty, Kelly, O'Kelly, McGuininess, McGuinn . . .

Chapter Eight

DREAMS AND THE PLANS LIFE MAKES FOR YOU

I returned home from my tour of the Azores like Sinatra descending on Manhattan after a triumphant run at the Sands.

I was on top of the world and confident that it was only a matter of time before it was my own name right next to Frank's on that neon marquee.

So, while my brothers and other kids in the neighborhood were grounded by preparations for this trade school or that job, my sights were fixed solely on the stars.

The great thing about being a kid is that you're allowed to indulge those crazy dreams.

The lousy thing about being a parent is that you often have to talk your child out of the crazy, without stripping away the dream.

That particular duty fell to my father. He took me off to the quiet of the kitchen and sat me down for a man-to-man talk. "You have a fine voice," he said.

I beamed, thinking this was the entirety of what he'd wanted to say.

> The lousy thing about being a parent is that you often have to talk your child out of the crazy, without stripping away the dream.

And then came the "*But* ..."

"But maybe you should think about—" He hesitated, searching for the words that would be strong enough to do the job he'd set out to accomplish, but gentle enough not to leave a scar.

His silence was all the time I needed. "Think about what?"

"College."

"College?"

He nodded. "College."

"But I'm going to be a singer. That's my dream."

He looked pained. "And dreams are important. They are. But they don't always come true, son. And even when they do, they're not necessarily the best thing to build your life on.

There are things that maybe you don't dream about when you're young, but those are the things that really fulfill you when you've grown to be a man."

None of this made sense to teenaged me. "Like what?"

"Like a family. When I was your age, do you think that my dream was to be a salesman in Scranton, Pennsylvania? Or maybe you think I didn't have any dreams at all?"

The truth was that I'd never really thought of my dad in that way, as having unrealized dreams or forgotten dreams or any dreams at all. He was just my dad.

"Of course I had dreams. Every young man does. And I promise you that they didn't include a wife and four kids. But those are the things that satisfy me most, that define me and give meaning to my life. So I'm not asking you to give up on your dreams, I'm not. I'm only suggesting that maybe you should prepare for a life that might come to mean even more, because that's what happened to me. I never realized my dreams, but in your mother and your brothers and you, I've found something that means so much more than any dream ever could."

> The truth was that I'd never really thought of my dad in that way, as having unrealized dreams or forgotten dreams or any dreams at all.

If I didn't understand why his eyes were misting, I understood his point. "College?"

He smiled and patted my hand. "I think that'd be a smart decision. You know, just in case."

Chapter Nine

SHOWTIME!

When it came to considering a future that didn't feature traveling the world as a singing sensation, my interest immediately turned to electrical engineering.

Yes, I realize that's quite a jump. And no, I can't quite explain that seemingly unconnected shift in interests.

I can only say with complete sincerity that within a very short period of time, my attention and passions became as focused on currents and amps as they had once been on harmonies and melodies.

There was just one problem.

Growing up, I was many things, but an academically distinguished student wasn't one of them. I was certainly no delinquent and I never made a failing grade, but

> **Within a very short period of time, my attention and passions became as focused on currents and amps as they had once been on harmonies and melodies.**

for some reason there was always something of a disconnect between the amount of effort I put into my studies (tremendous) and the grades that I earned as a result (mediocre).

Growing up, I was many things, but an academically distinguished student wasn't one of them.

So when it came time to apply to college in order to pursue my newfound interest in electrical engineering, my application to the University of Scranton's engineering department left more than a little lacking and was answered with a thin envelope and a "We regret to inform you …"

And suddenly, almost overnight, I found myself in the unenviable situation of needing a backup plan for my backup plan.

I thought for a while what that might be, but came back again and again to electrical engineering. And so I decided that what I would do, rather than making an alternate plan, was to dedicate myself to making my plan work by sheer force of will.

Easier said than done.

The University of Scranton is a distinguished Jesuit institution in the city's Hill Section.

As a mere high schooler, I was awed and (maybe) a little intimidated in the campus surroundings, but I was set in my purpose and marched straight to the university's Office of Admissions.

The dean of admission was Father McGee, a man who looked as if he'd been put behind his massive desk by Hollywood casting.

"Mister Holleran," he greeted me, in the way that only a Jesuit can use the honorific "mister" to assert their complete authority.

I took the seat he offered.

"And what is it you think I can do for you?"

I took a deep breath and thought back to all of those lessons my mother had me take.

Showtime!

"I've applied for the electrical engineering program," I said and flashed a smile.

Ta-da!

He was completely unimpressed. "I know."

I took another deep breath and prepared for the encore I could tell he didn't want. "I was wondering if there was any way—"

"I'm afraid your grades simply weren't good enough for admission into our program."

"But if you could only make an exception—"

"I don't think you understand, Mr. Holleran. This isn't a matter of exceptions—which I'm not in the habit of making. I simply wouldn't be doing you any favor in admitting you to a program in which you would find the course work too difficult. You simply couldn't complete the program. That's all."

I was raised to respect my elders and revere the clergy, but I have never been able to countenance anyone telling me that I couldn't do something.

"Oh, yes, I could." The words were out of my mouth before I had the opportunity to temper the defiance of their tone.

He looked at me across that desk for the longest thirty seconds of my life. If possible, he looked even sterner. "People who sit in that chair usually don't talk to me like that, Mr. Holleran. Those that do either suffer from an overabundance of confidence or a deficit of common sense. Which do you suppose is your affliction?"

I thought about it for a moment and answered as honestly as I could. "I suppose a bit of both."

And then the impossible happened.

He smiled. "I'll tell you what, Mr. Holleran. I'll give you your chance. Although I'm certain that you'll regret it and be gone and forgotten long before the school year is over."

I got to my feet. "I promise you I won't."

I thanked him and got out of the room before he had a chance to change his mind.

When I arrived home, I told my mother and father what I'd done and explained all about the new program I'd be entering in the fall like it was my own personal accomplishment.

Looking back at it now, I wish instead that I'd thanked them. If it hadn't been for my mother, I wouldn't have had the confidence I needed to have talked my way into the program.

And if not for my father, I might have been singing in some dismal dinner theater in Peoria or somewhere even worse.

They were both right. I wish I'd told them that at the time.

Chapter Ten

A PROMISE MADE IS
A DEBT UNPAID

It's amazing how quickly a triumph can turn into something completely different.

I was still glowing from having convinced Father McGee to give me a chance at the engineering program when I ran headfirst into the brick wall that was ... well, the engineering program.

College represented for me a whole new academic experience. I had been given a wonderful educational foundation by those nuns at parochial school, and I'm grateful to them for that, but the Jesuits were something altogether different.

The program was centered on science and mathematics, but there was English literature and history and philosophy, as well.

Any one of the courses would have presented a challenge, but taken together ... well, taken all together, it seemed to create an insurmountable obstacle for me ... a brick wall.

I worked as hard as I could, but every one of those subjects demanded that I work even harder. I lost sleep and skipped meals. I drank coffee. I worried about failing and about disappointing my parents.

> I worked as hard as I could, but every one of those subjects demanded that I work even harder.

It was a miserable time, and more than anything, I just wanted it to be over.

Yet it seemed an odd coincidence that whenever the thought of quitting crossed my mind for more than a moment or two, I would unexpectedly find myself crossing paths with Father McGee.

> It seemed an odd coincidence that whenever the thought of quitting crossed my mind for more than a moment or two, I would unexpectedly find myself crossing paths with Father McGee.

"Good day, Mr. Holleran."

"Dean."

"How are you?"

"Fine," I would lie.

He'd usually just nod, but in that simple gesture I knew he was holding me to a promise I'd made to him.

And to my parents.

But most of all to myself.

And somehow I did it. Or at least, I made it through that first year and qualified to sit for my final exams.

Everything depended on those grades, and the time I spent waiting was even worse than the time spent working. When I was studying, at least there was something to do. Now that it was all over, the only thing I could do was wait to see whether I'd lived up to that promise I'd made.

Chapter Eleven

THAT DAY

I was alone in the room that I shared with my brothers when a knock came at the door.

It was my mother, and her eyes were brighter than I had ever seen them before. A smile lit her face. In her hands was an envelope, and she offered it like she was giving me a gift. "This came for you."

It was from the university. A notice. My grades.

My heart raced and my hands trembled as I tore the envelope open.

After all of the struggle, all of the hard work, I had not only survived my freshman year, I had managed something far, far more. I had succeeded. I had made the Dean's List.

And though the marks were right there on the paper, I couldn't quite believe they were real until I looked up at my mother and saw her nod her head softly, her eyes even brighter now, her smiler wider.

I had never seen my mother looking quite so proud as she did in that moment.

And I never saw her again.

I had never seen my mother looking quite so proud as she did in that moment.

She died later that same day of a heart attack brought on by the aftereffects of the rheumatic fever she had as a child.

And I am not exaggerating or being overly sentimental to say that some part of me died with her.

Some part of my brothers, too.

And almost all of my father.

My mother was the heart of the Hollerans, and without her there in our midst, there seemed to be no more life left in any of us.

Chapter Twelve

HILLTOP MANOR, UNIT 29H

A pall fell over that once happy house on Prospect Avenue, a dark cloud of despair that did not lift or abate.

There were family and friends who came to visit us in the aftermath of my mother's passing. They brought casseroles in Pyrex pans and well-intended promises that "everything will get better with time."

They were wrong.

Very wrong.

There are some people—most, maybe—who come into this world, wander their way here and there, and then leave again all on their own, without ever really touching or being touched by anyone in a lasting and meaningful way.

And then there are others who seem like they were only born into this world for the purpose of finding their other half—for finding, as the Irish call it, their *Anam Cara*.

Their soulmate.

My mother and father were like that.

Without my mother by his side, my father was like a man without a heart. Or a soul. He was left just a hollow husk of the debonair man who'd always had a twinkle in his eye and been quick with a joke that brought a smile to everyone's face whether it was funny or not.

He lost everything with her passing, including the ability to hang onto the life that they'd built together.

In the void she left behind, he lost his job, the meager savings they'd managed to squirrel away, and finally, that small house on Prospect Avenue, which was the only home that any of us had ever known.

Everything.

In fact, if anything, the situation for the Holleran men only grew darker and the burden of her loss heavier with each day that passed without her.

And the brunt of that weight fell on my shoulders.

Or at least that is how it seemed to me then.

My mother had made a life out of taking care of her husband and sons in a way that was entirely unique to each of them.

Without her there was … nothing.

And someone had to fill that void.

That someone was me.

My older brother, Jack, was already off in the Air Force by this time.

My brothers, Charlie and Jim, were younger than me by three and five years, respectively, and not yet of an age to take care of themselves, much less to help me hold together the pieces of our crumbling family.

And that left me to be mother and father to two boys who needed both.

I tended to the house and the various needs of my father and brothers. I tried to keep meals on the table and my younger brothers in school.

I tried to keep my father from falling apart any further.

Replacing my mother would have been impossible for anyone, but for a young man beginning his sophomore year at university it was something even worse.

My grades suffered.

My family suffered.

Everything suffered.

And with no place else to turn, the lot of us ended up in public housing.

To say there was a shock involved in the move would be a serious understatement. We not only lost the house that still echoed with the lilt of my mother's voice and the laughter of the life we'd all known with her, but also a larger community in the neighborhood and parish that had been every bit the home as the four walls and roof on Prospect Avenue had been.

Once we had been "The Hollerans from over on Prospect Avenue," and that had meant something that each and every one of us had treasured.

Now we were just the most recent lost souls to join a collective for other lost souls.

Now we were just "those guys in Hilltop Manor, Unit 29H."

That designation brought with it a lot of unexpected baggage. For South Scranton—hell, all of Scranton, all of America, even— an address in public housing carried with it a sense of shame and unwanted (and unwarranted) personal identification.

Many of my classmates came from the grand homes along the oak-lined streets of the city's stately Green Ridge section or Hill Section, and the least of them made an effort to make me aware of that, too.

There was no need. I already understood the differences between us.

Adversity is a funny thing. My time split between Hilltop Manor and the university taught me a lot about its effects—and unintended consequences.

For some people, those types of challenges create an anchor that weighs them down in life and prevents them from ever moving forwards from their situation. Overwhelmed with despair, they sink further and further into listlessness and too often into the sort of negative behaviors that only make bad situations worse.

But for others, adversity is like metallic hydrogen—the most powerful rocket fuel known to man.

There wasn't a day I spent at Hilltop Manor that I wasn't grateful for the roof over my head and painfully conscious of the tragic fact that there were multitudes all around me who did not even share that good fortune. But at the same time, I never spent a night under that roof that wasn't marked by my determination to do the work necessary to get me out of that situation and to ensure that I never, ever went back.

I never spent a night under that roof that wasn't marked by my determination to do the work necessary to get me out of that situation and to ensure that I never, ever went back.

I am not so naïve to suppose that this world is a fair one or that opportunities and circumstances are as balanced for all of us as they should be. (Life has taught me that lesson directly.)

But much of what encompasses an individual's life is what they are willing to accept, combined with whatever effort they are willing to expend to achieve change.

No matter the losses I'd suffered, I was never willing to allow them to dictate my future.

And with the vision of what my life would be one day fixed in my mind, I was never once too tired or otherwise engaged that I didn't commit my total energies to making that my reality.

Some of our paths are rockier and steeper than others, but every determined hiker can reach the summit.

I know of no one who exemplifies this principle better than my younger brothers, Charles and Jim, who spent more of their formative years at Hilltop Manor than I did. I think the darkness of those times weighed more heavily on them, too. Still, they shared my determination that one day they would put all of that behind them.

> **With the vision of what my life would be one day fixed in my mind, I was never once too tired or otherwise engaged that I didn't commit my total energies to making that my reality.**

And that's exactly what they did.

Jim had a distinguished career at IBM followed by a series of executive assignments at Computer Associates. He and his wife, Sandra, who live in New York City, were always the cool couple looked up to by all their nieces and nephews.

Jim was the go-to guy for his brothers' children when there was an embarrassing teenage question they were reluctant to ask their parents.

Charles put his significant talents to work and followed his own path to success. He enjoyed a long and distinguished career, eventually rising to become the chief corporate communications officer for Coca-Cola, and then for Ford.

He and his former wife MaryJane have a wonderful family and three terrific children: Michelle, Kevin and Renee.

He's made a tremendous success of his life.

Some time ago, Charles and his current wife, Kathryn, built a home in the Berkshires, a well-known vacation destination in western Massachusetts dotted with quaint villages and rustic resorts. The area is populated primarily by those young Turks looking for some seasonal retreat from the "fast track" and retired executives without any intention of ever going back.

It's a beautiful place, and their home there is a warm and welcoming place for his family and friends.

It's also a brick-and-mortar testament to the many achievements he's made in his life—and the obstacles he's had to overcome to earn them.

When guests come to visit and turn off the main road to start up the long drive to Charlie's place, just off to the left there's a sign that reads: Hilltop Manor, Unit 29H.

I'm certain most of his visitors never take any notice of it, or have any understanding of its meaning if they do.

But my brothers and me, we always take note.

And we all understand.

Chapter Thirteen

SHE'S THE ONE

In the wake of losing my mother, I was rescued from my despair by the one woman who was capable of showing me a joy in life I'd thought I'd lost forever.

I first met Kathy Jordan when we were both in high school.

The first time I laid my eyes on her smiling face, I knew that she was the one for me. I know that may sound clichéd, but that doesn't make it less true.

My friends were quick to tell me that she came with some baggage: A boyfriend. A quarterback. The jealous type.

Now, I'm no tough guy. Never have been, never will be. And I've never felt any shame about that fact.

I also have never been in the habit of courting trouble, especially back in the days when the sort of beating that today would been seen as felonious aggravated assault and an accompanying civil suit was regarded as nothing more than an incident of "boys will be boys."

Still, there are some truly rare prizes in this world that are more than worth a good ass-kicking, and even from afar I was absolutely certain that a moment of Kathy Jordan's time was one of those things.

I walked right up to her.

She was more surprised than impressed. "Yes?"

There are some truly rare prizes in this world that are more than worth a good ass-kicking.

"I'm Marty Holleran."

She smiled. "Kathy. Kathy Jordan."

We talked for a bit, mostly me nervously trying to coax some conversation from her and then her being amused by my flustered efforts.

I have lived a life that is largely free of regrets, but let me confess one of them right now.

In those days there was a drive-in where teens congregated called Kay's. I'd like to say that what happened next was simply the result of being stunned by her smile, but the explanation is that I was probably way out of my class.

Anyway, I summoned all my suave and said, "So, Kay, would you like to go to Kay's?"

(Recalling the line pains me even now.)

"Don't call me Kay." It turned out my attempt to create a sense of familiarity with my own little nickname only reminded her of a distant cousin named Kay who was unattractive, overweight, and nasty. Her smile disappeared.

And despite that cheesy line, she's been at my side ever since.

She got me through those dark days when otherwise I would have been swallowed up by my hopelessness. She was my North Star when otherwise I would have lost my way in the dark.

Chapter Fourteen

SHINE ON

Nothing got easier in the year that followed my mother's passing. Not the second year, either, or the third. Not really.

But I must admit that each year brought changes, little by little.

And if the Holleran men were all still mourning and managing in our respective ways, at least time went by.

My senior year of college. Fall was just beginning to express its intentions of turning to winter. I came in late from a date with Kathy, not necessarily glad to be home, but grateful for the warmth I found there.

The place was dark and silent, and I was thankful for that, too.

I took a seat at the kitchen table.

My father appeared out of the shadows. "You have a good time?"

"I did. I always do with Kathy."

He took a seat. "That's important. It's the woman that makes the man. And a good woman will make any man great. Just look at me and your mother. Everything I am was all her making." He hung his head. "Just look at me now without her."

We were both silent for a moment.

And then I felt compelled to say aloud what had been on my mind for a long time. "I think I want to marry her, Dad."

He pushed his own sadness far enough away to offer me a smile. "I think you should."

I was grateful for his approval, but wanting to marry Kathy was a long way from being financially positioned to do so.

"When are you going to pop the question?"

I shrugged and shook my head. "I don't even have the money for a ring."

"Is that all that's stopping you?"

It seemed like more than enough.

"Well, that's reasonable," he said. "But there's no room for reason where love is concerned. There's always going to be this or that standing in the way, but if it's love—really love—then you've got to put all of that aside and find a way."

There's always going to be this or that standing in the way, but if it's love—really love—then you've got to put all of that aside and find a way.

"It is love," I said.

"Then you'll find a way."

He got up from the table and left me there with my thoughts, my worries, and foolish calculations about what I could do—or do without—to somehow scrape together the money for the ring I knew Kathy deserved.

I was so lost in those thoughts that I was startled when my father reappeared from the shadows. He retook his seat without a word.

He braced himself, teetering closer to that emotional edge than I had seen him in a long while.

I wasn't sure what had upset him so much, but hoped that raising the issue of getting married hadn't reopened his wounds.

Without a word, he took my hand and put something inside, curling my fingers around it, and then holding my hand firmly in his for a moment.

When he let go, I opened my hand. On my palm was a small, worn ring box. I knew immediately what was inside, but somehow I was still surprised to open it and find my mother's engagement ring shining there.

I looked to him.

He nodded, fighting back tears.

I didn't bother to resist mine. "Are you sure?"

"Your mother would've had me do it a long time ago."

"Dad …" If I'd had words to speak, my voice certainly would've failed me, but at that moment I didn't have either one.

"If she makes you half as happy as your mother made me, then you're going to have a wonderful life and that's all your mother ever wanted for you."

I took my mother's ring and gave it to Kathy later that year.

She said "Yes" when I asked her, and every day since she has made my life even more wonderful than even my mother could have hoped for.

Chapter Fifteen

IN THE ARMY NOW

1964 was a hard year.

Not just personally for the Hollerans, but for America.

The collective memories of World War II had not faded completely, and the private nightmares of Korea were still fresh with too many of the young men who had returned home from that conflict. We were a nation haunted by the endless series of wars that seemed to have consumed the century, and yet the prospect of still more conflicts seemed inevitable.

We had just breathed a collective sigh of relief after the Cuban Missile Crisis, when the grief of losing President Kennedy shook us to our core. And in all the global turmoil, there were rumblings of more war on the way, including a skirmish in a little corner of southeast Asia, a former French colony known as Vietnam.

When I had begun college four years earlier, the Army ROTC program seemed like the only way to handle what otherwise would have been the impossibly high costs of a higher education. At graduation, however, the ramifications of that decision weighed a little heavier.

Don't get me wrong, I have never for a minute regretted my decision to join the Army, and I am proud of my service, but when you are just twenty-one years old, a recent college graduate, and newly engaged, the reality of impending military service hits you with an unexpected gravitas.

> When you are just twenty-one years old, a recent college graduate, and newly engaged, the reality of impending military service hits you with an unexpected gravitas.

And at the same time that I was commissioned as an officer in the U.S. Army and considering the prospect of leaving for Southeast Asia, I received another honor from my country: NASA offered me a full fellowship to receive my master's degree at the University of Delaware.

The dilemma of obligation and opportunity was difficult for me to navigate, but in the end the decision was made for me. The Army issued me a deferment from active duty, and that meant that I could continue my education.

Life had shown me tragedy and challenges, to be sure, but I don't think I ever felt the weight of a decision quite so heavily before.

Chapter Sixteen

A MISSING PIECE

The University of Delaware had a beautiful campus.

There was always something going on.

And I got to enjoy almost none of it.

I was there on a NASA fellowship, which meant that if I didn't maintain a B average or better, I was out on the street—and I knew what that meant.

Even though the educational fundamentals I had developed during my four years at the University of Scranton had provided a foundation that made my graduate coursework relatively easy, I was still driven by that gnawing sense of needing to work harder that the Jesuits had instilled in me.

But that wasn't what had me so out of sorts and generally miserable.

What truly made those days so difficult was that I was alone—or rather, without Kathy.

I had left for Delaware, but my heart had stayed with her back in Scranton.

Long-distance relationships are always challenging, but in those prehistoric times before FaceTime and other technological fixes, the endless days without her presence in my life became increasingly difficult and finally impossible.

We had planned to wait to get married until after I finished my schooling.

We had planned lots of things, but what I hadn't planned on was how unmanageable my life was without her.

We were married in January.

After a brief honeymoon in the Poconos—at that time the "Honeymoon Capital of the World"—we returned to Delaware together.

We made the trip in a Volkswagen Beetle that required a quick sign of the cross and whispered word to the Blessed Mother every time you turned the key. I think we had a little over three hundred dollars in our pocket, most of it still in gift envelopes given to us at our wedding.

It's crazy to think of it now, but I'm telling you that we didn't have a worry or care in the world.

We were young and in love—and we were together. Forever.

I'm telling you that we didn't have a worry or care in the world. We were young and in love—and we were together. Forever.

And that is when my life really began.

It was a wonderful adventure for us to begin as a newlywed couple.

And we're still living that wonderful adventure today.

Chapter Seventeen

THE GREATEST ADVENTURE OF THEM ALL

Someone once told me that you don't know anything before you have a child.

Nothing.

You think you know all about love and hope and fear. You think you understand the myriad of emotions that make up the human condition. You think you understand.

You don't.

It's not until your first child that you realize how much love your heart will hold.

It's not until your first child that you realize how much love your heart will hold.

Or how strong your hope for the future is, not necessarily your own, but for a person you've only just met.

And no matter what fire you've walked through in your life, it is not until you've held your first child that you can understand the true depths of fear to which your heart and soul can plummet in simply considering something going wrong now.

Ten and a half months after Kathy and I were married, our son Marty was born.

And it was as if I came into a brand new world with him.

Everything changed with his blessed arrival.

I might not have really understood before, but with our baby in my arms and Kathy beaming up at me, I was suddenly very certain about almost everything.

Chapter Eighteen

THE EQUATION OF MOTION AND OTHER THINGS I LEARNED

Among the things I became absolutely certain about after the birth of Marty was that I was going to provide him as perfect a life as I possibly could. His mother, too, of course.

After receiving my master's degree in electrical engineering from the University of Delaware, I had the opportunity to continue my studies and earn a doctorate degree. It was a wonderful opportunity, and at a different time in my life the prospect of becoming Dr. Marty Holleran would have been the fulfillment of ambitions I had barely dared to dream.

But I was a husband and a father now, and my goals had changed. My responsibilities, too.

Coming out of the University of Delaware, I had a number of interesting job offers—and absolutely no idea how to evaluate them and determine which offered me the best overall opportunity.

Of all of those prospects, one of the most promising was with IBM, which at the time was leading the way into the brave new world of computing. My interview with them went very well, but each representative I met with seemed very impressed with themselves.

Early in the morning, I met with someone from their engineering department who asked me what I knew about the equation of motion. Before I could confess "Very little," he had filled the whiteboard behind his desk with a series of elaborate equations that expressed his own mastery of the concept.

I pretended to be impressed.

This must have been the Equation of the Day on their corporate campus, because later in the day I had a meeting with the senior member of the department, who made his own reference to equation of motion formulas, implying with his tone that such a calculation was beyond someone like me.

I smiled and then, without a word, proceeded to the whiteboard and proceeded to write out the same formula I'd seen his colleague write out just a few hours earlier.

His eyes bugged and his jaw dropped.

He made an offer on the spot.

And that was the moment I learned that it's not necessarily all about what you know—sometimes it's about what they think you know.

And what I knew at that time was that I was never going to be happy at IBM.

It's not necessarily all about what you know—sometimes it's about what they think you know.

It was (and is) a wonderful company. Everyone who had interviewed me was certainly at the forefront of their industry. What they floated past me was a flattering offer that would have provided me with some really dynamic opportunities and a compensation package that would've gone a long way toward providing the life I wanted to give to Kathy and Marty. On paper, it was perfect.

But I didn't feel any chemistry, either with the company or the people.

And without the right chemistry, nothing ever works out.

General Electric, however, was a completely different situation.

Like IBM, GE was an iconic American company, at the top of its industry and breaking new ground every day. And what they'd included in their offer certainly indicated that they saw my potential. I was offered a position on the advanced Manufacturing Management Program.

But it was more than just the generous offer that made the decision for GE a no-brainer for me.

The minute I walked into the place, I just felt at home. The representatives I spoke to were every bit as sharp and on top of their game as anyone else I'd interviewed with, but they were also grounded in a way that made it clear they were real people.

And that's who I wanted to work for and with. Real people.

That was the total basis of my foundation.

> That's who I wanted to work for and with. Real people.

Kathy and I loaded up what few belongings we had in our student housing, strapped Marty into his car seat, and hit the road headed north.

Next stop: Johnson City.

Chapter Nineteen

FIRST STEPS

Johnson City is one-third of the Triple Cities, along with Binghamton and Endicott, in Upstate New York.

That's only about an hour from Scranton, just sixty miles north up I-81, and that proximity made Kathy and me feel immediately at home. What made it even better was the fact that Kathy's sister, AnnMarie, and her husband, Ed Janeski, one of my best friends, and their family lived nearby.

We found our new neighbors to be no-nonsense people, but grounded in the same principles that we had been raised with. And it was those same fundamentals that I relied on in that first entry in the working world.

All of the other new corporate hires at GE were eager to find office jobs, but I was ready to roll up my sleeves and get to work, so my first assignment was as a manager of a production line.

It was an admittedly unorthodox choice for someone who'd just left grad school with a master's in electrical engineering, but there were two distinct advantages to the position.

The first was that it exposed me to a side of the company that not many others—and certainly none of my fellow recent hires—got a chance to see. As engineers, we all knew that everything begins with an idea put to paper, but I was interested to see how those designs were transformed into an actual product. It was, in a way, an opportunity for me to "reverse engineer" the entire process.

> As engineers, we all knew that everything begins with an idea put to paper, but I was interested to see how those designs were transformed into an actual product.

The other advantage that my position in production afforded me was the opportunity to be a supervisor right off the bat. I supervised thirty workers on the line, and that was a unique situation for a new hire and an opportunity to demonstrate leadership skills straight out of the gate.

It was not a glamorous position, but from my first day on the job, I was determined that I would do everything asked of me—and a lot of things that weren't.

When management wanted to put together an employee golf tournament, I was the guy organizing tee times. And while many of my coworkers shook their heads and told me that this didn't have anything to do with engineering, I quietly continued to demonstrate that I was a guy who could get things done.

Whatever needed to be done.

And while there were a few "extra" assignments that I didn't necessarily relish, I focused on the opportunity in all of them.

Maybe my favorite experience was an evening spent escorting Billy Ray "The Rabbit" Smith, who had just retired after leading the Baltimore Colts to a victory against the Dallas Cowboys in Super Bowl V. He was the guest of honor at a GE-sponsored dinner, and I was given the task of escorting him during his stay in Johnson City.

When the dinner was over and I was taking him back to his hotel, he suggested that we stop for a drink instead. I ordered a glass of Scotch. He asked for the whole bottle.

We talked for a while, and he told me that as the leader of the Colt's defense they had one goal and that was to shut out their opponent. Nothing fancy, just prevent them from scoring.

That's it.

"That's the only way to live your life," he said.

I was a long way from the NFL, but I understood.

He looked around the bar I'd picked. "This is a classy place. Nice and quiet. But you'd be surprised how many times I go out for a drink and there's some asshole who wants to fight me just because I'm Rabbit Smith."

Now, Billy Ray was 6'3" and an easy 250. His face was twisted and busted, suggesting he was no stranger to pain. His hands were massive and callused, evidence that he had dealt out more than his share of pain, too. Fighting didn't seem like a reasonable angle to pursue with a man like that. "You're kidding me."

He shook his head. "Just last week I was in a bar with some friends, minding my own business, and this guy came up to me. 'You're Billy Ray Smith, huh?' I nodded. He said, 'You don't look so tough to me. I think I can kick your ass.'"

"What did you do?"

"I told him, 'For the better part of twenty years, I played on the defensive line. And every snap of the ball, I only had one desire.

I didn't want to tackle anyone. I didn't want to hurt anyone. I just wanted to kill them. So you go outside with me, you better be goddamn certain you can kick my ass because if I go out there with you, I go out there to kill you.'"

"What did he do?"

"What most of them do, he turned around and went back off to his little life." Rabbit threw back another glass of Scotch. "I get asked to step out a lot, but very few guys are willing to go. And that's the secret to life. I don't care whether you're on the defensive line during the Super Bowl or you're—" He looked at me. "What do you do?"

"I'm an engineer."

"Good, an engineer. Doesn't matter what you do. The secret to life is that you do it as goddamn hard as you can."

Every day I went into work and I supervised that production line just as goddamn hard as I could.

I toasted my new friend, because I knew that he spoke the truth.

And I took those words to heart.

Every day I went into work and I supervised that production line just as goddamn hard as I could.

And so my new family and I quickly settled into a wonderful routine.

I was happy in my new job, and every day brought confirmation that I'd made the right selection in choosing to come to GE. Kathy was content at home, and Marty seemed to be growing bigger every day. It was a perfect little moment in life.

That should have given me reason to suspect that change was in the offing.

But it didn't.

So I was caught completely off guard when I came home one day and found a letter waiting for me.

The sender was U.S. Army.

The recipient was Second Lieutenant Martin J. Holleran.

Chapter Twenty

THE TAPESTRY OF LIFE

It was my duty to go.

It was my honor to serve.

But saying good-bye to Kathy and Marty was among the hardest things I've ever had to do in my life. I left them both with promises that everything would be all right, but in my heart I was aware of other possibilities.

I hugged them both all the more tightly.

The notice from the Army directed me to report to signal school at Fort Gordon, Georgia.

This was 1966.

President Johnson had just escalated the American presence in Vietnam, and all of my fellow officers who arrived with me to begin their active duty shared an unspoken understanding of what the future might hold. We attended our classes and got our work done. There was never a minute when we were less than professional in the completion of our duties.

At the same time, we were human beings—young men just entering the prime of our lives. None of us expressed the fear we felt, but every one of us felt it.

At the conclusion of signal school, we all got our assignments. Most of my classmates were deployed directly to Vietnam.

I was one of the rare exceptions.

Someone up the chain of command had taken notice of my engineering background and decided I would be of greater service elsewhere.

The point of this particular exercise, writing my memoir, was for me to put my life experiences down on paper. This moment, however, was so emotionally complex that it still eludes being captured and conveyed by words.

There was, of course, a feeling of elation in knowing that I would soon be reunited with Kathy and Marty.

But whatever personal joy that moment contained for me was immediately tempered by the devastating realization that so many of my classmates were facing a drastically different future. To many people, I suppose this outcome might have seemed like a stroke of great fortune (and I know that it was) but it came with a terrible price, a nagging sense of remorse that darkened many of those days and stays with me still.

Life is funny.

> Whatever personal joy that moment contained for me was immediately tempered by the devastating realization that so many of my classmates were facing a drastically different future.

On one hand, it's amazing how simple life can be when it comes down to being sent to war or directed otherwise. Go or stay home—it doesn't get any simpler than that.

But on the other hand, it's amazing how intricate the intertwining patterns are within the tapestry of our lives. Being an engineer had saved my life—or at least saved me from Vietnam, which seemed to me then to be the same thing.

I thought of the conversation I'd had with my father, when he'd suggested I find a place in college.

> It's amazing how intricate the intertwining patterns are within the tapestry of our lives.

I thought of Father McGee, who never made exceptions but did for me.

I thought of my mother, who gave me the confidence (and the gift of gab) to persuade him that he should do so.

And I thought of where I would've been if dozens of other people hadn't intervened in one way or another over the course of my life. The thousands of interactions that had led me there.

Life is, indeed, funny.

Chapter Twenty-One

THE GREATEST RESPONSIBILITY, THE GRIMMEST TASK

My assignment was to Fort Monmouth, New Jersey, where I was supposed to be working in their test labs. And I did put in time there. It was an enriching professional opportunity for a young engineer.

Still, my duties as a soldier were greater than just those of a research scientist, and the extra responsibilities were even more impactful in shaping me as a man than I ever could have anticipated.

There was a shortage of officers on base, and so we were frequently called to fulfill an assortment of other obligations beyond the most logical assignments. Of these, the greatest responsibility—and grimmest task—was participating in Military Death Notification.

To this day I can remember every assignment I was given, every house I visited, every person I informed. I can close my eyes and see myself back there in that place and time like it was happening still.

They know, of course, why you have come.

The parents.

The wives.

The children.

Before the military sedan has even pulled to the curb, a dozen other homes in the neighborhood have spotted that ominous car, breathed a guilty sigh of relief as it passed, and pulled their curtains against the truth they all know it contains.

And then you arrive.

The sedan parks. And you can feel the driver's relief, gratitude for the first time all day that he is not the officer sitting in the back.

You open the door and step out into the day and take stock of your surroundings as if you were entering a foreign landscape.

Sometimes the streets are empty. Other times there are children at play or men mowing lawns. But no matter who else is around and no matter the time of day, you are always surrounded by an unnatural quiet.

The car door closing behind you sounds like a shot.

The scraping sound of your dress shoe soles against the grit on the sidewalk.

The thump of your footsteps ascending the porch stairs.

Your knock on the door echoes in that hellish quiet.

And then someone whose day was perfectly normal just five seconds before you arrived pulls open the front door and sees you standing there in your dress uniform.

They start to shake and their eyes open wide, filled with all of the horror and sorrow that you are there to deliver to them.

Because, as I said, they know.

They all know.

And you cannot show that their grief is your grief, too. You have no right to claim even the smallest piece of that for your own. That is theirs and theirs alone.

Instead, you stand, tall and straight and unmoved. You are a soldier. And you tell them that they have lost one of their own.

Then someone whose day was perfectly normal just five seconds before you arrived pulls open the front door and sees you standing there in your dress uniform.

But you must always keep to yourself that you have, too.

Your voice does not break, your eyes cannot tear.

You are a soldier.

And one of your brothers will not be coming home.

Not ever again.

You give them the condolences of the secretary of the Army, but what compensation is that for a son? A husband? A father?

What compensation could there possibly be?

They have all lost someone.

And more than that, they have lost something within themselves, something that can never be replaced.

You have, too. But you keep that to yourself.

Chapter Twenty-Two

THE DIFFERENCE BETWEEN A THREAT AND A PROMISE

The Military Death Notification wasn't my only additional assignment. And it certainly wasn't the only one that far outside my own personal wheelhouse.

Today, any criminal matters occurring within the Army's jurisdiction are adjudicated by trained legal professionals through the Judge Advocate General's Corps (JAG Corps). In 1966, however, there was a shortage of officers in Fort Monmouth, and any one of us could be called on to serve in any capacity. Adjudicator. Prosecutor. Defense counsel. The applicability of our credentials didn't particularly matter to my superiors.

Given all that, some might think that my training as an engineer would have led me to pursue the cases assigned to me in an emotionally detached and logically ordered fashion. And under normal circumstances, I'd say that was a fairly solid assumption.

But there were notable exceptions.

Now, I try to be accepting of people. All people. Live and let live, I say. But I do have my limits, and there are a few qualities or personality traits that I simply can't tolerate.

One of them is casual cruelty.

I cannot abide a bully. I never could. I still can't.

I cannot abide a bully. I never could. I still can't.

And so, of all the criminal cases I was asked to handle in my ill-fitting position as a legal representative, the one that impacted me most strongly then still reverberates with me today.

It was a simple matter. Or, at least, it had started out that way.

A soldier, a combat vet, had just come back from his tour of Vietnam, and his "Welcome Home!" celebrations had gotten a little out of hand. He and his friends had been picked up by some over-zealous MPs. (If you ask me, the MPs should've just shaken their hands with gratitude for their service and given them a ride back to the barracks to sober up.) Once the group got locked up in the guardhouse, however, a simple matter quickly got complicated.

Very complicated.

The first time I met my new client, I was struck by how young he looked. Just a kid.

Except for his eyes.

They were the oldest eyes I'd ever looked into.

And the right one had a distinctive purplish mark around it.

"Someone surprised you with a left?" I asked as I took my seat.

The kid touched his shiner. "Surprised nothing, his buddy was holding me back."

"How's that?"

The story he told me made my blood boil.

He'd been out with some friends and they all freely admitted to having had a beer or two too many. Maybe eight too many. They got loud and louder, and sooner or later someone got annoyed and called the MPs.

But the kid hadn't gotten the black eye on the street. They were rowdy, but not fighting. The shiner had come once they were locked up.

There was a sergeant, a guard, who seemed to hone in on the young soldiers almost as soon as the bars had clanged shut behind them. The sergeant had a buddy, and the two of them went on taunting the young soldiers, saying things that no one should have to listen to—especially not combat veterans just returned home.

At some point, the sergeant and his cohort went from hurling insults to throwing punches.

To protect himself and his friends, the kid hauled off and clocked the loudmouthed bully.

As I said, it should've been a simple matter of a bully getting what he had coming to him, but there was just one problem: the guard was a sergeant and my client was just a private. And in the Army, rank is everything.

I told the kid that everything would be all right, but I didn't let on that hitting a superior—even one who deserved it—was a very serious offense in the Army.

Many-years-in-Leavenworth serious.

I've always been fairly direct in my approach to problems, and so I went straight to the sergeant. I found him on duty, and he was actually laughing about the incident with one of his cronies, who I assumed was the other creep involved. They were making jokes about the fate waiting for the kid once he got to Leavenworth.

I wasn't amused. "It just so happens I'm here to talk to you about that particular soldier."

The sergeant was surprised his comments had been overheard, and he leaned forward in his chair. "What about him?"

"Don't you rise for an officer?" I asked.

He looked to his friend.

"He's only a corporal," I observed. "I'm the only officer on the floor. So, I'm going to ask you again: Don't you rise for an officer?"

He slowly, deliberately got to his feet. "Yes, sir." *Sarcasm.*

"I talked to that soldier," I said. "He told me that you instigated the situation, harassed and threatened him and his friends."

"Oh, I don't know about that." He snuck a smirk to his friend, but I caught it, too.

"I've got witnesses who do."

"Witnesses?"

"Yes."

"Well—"

"Do you know what the penalty is for giving false testimony before a sworn tribunal?" I wasn't exactly certain myself, but I figured it must be severe.

Fortunately, he didn't either. He shook his head and his jaw drooped a little.

"Do you know what the charge is for bringing a false accusation before a sworn tribunal?" I asked.

Two for two.

His mouth dropped all the way open, and his eyes bulged. "Relax, relax. I'll drop the charges." He offered me an insincere smile as a settlement.

"I know you will. I'm not worried about my client." My voice was steady and sure.

The sergeant hadn't quite put the pieces together yet. "Then who you worried about?"

"I'm worried about the next time."

"Who said there's going to be a next time?" he asked.

"With guys like you, there's always a next time." I said.

I'd touched a nerve, and he showed me just a sample of what my client had seen up close.

"I think you better watch yourself," he said.

"Is that a threat? Do you know what the charge is for threatening an officer?"

"What are you getting so excited about?"

"I'll tell you what's not a threat," I said. "I'm not going to let you do this to another soldier ever again. And I'm going to make sure that you pay for every soldier you've already done it to."

"And how you think you going to do that?" It was as much of a threat as he dared to make towards an officer.

I just smiled. "You're bigger than me."

"Yeah, I am."

"And tougher."

"Finally, we agree on something."

"But I'm way smarter. I'm going to go back and do my homework, and when I'm done I'm going to hang you out to dry."

And as I said, that wasn't a threat. It was a promise. And one I meant to keep.

I went back to the JAG Corps offices, rolled up my sleeves, and did a little digging through the files. What I found was that sergeant's name, over and over again. Same situation.

But tragically for those other soldiers I hadn't represented, a very different outcome.

I called the matter to the attention of my superiors and filed a formal complaint. When I was done, I'd kept that promise. And I'm proud to say that when all was said and done it was that sergeant, not my client, who wound up doing a stretch in Leavenworth.

Chapter Twenty-Three

ALWAYS SMILE

Of course, not all of my time in the military was taken up with serious issues.

There were other times that I still remember with a smile.

I remember I was scheduled to make a trip to Germany. My orders came through on a Monday, and this being the military, I was supposed to be in Germany by Friday. Not a lot of time for packing and prepping.

Now, going to Germany for the first time was a big deal for me, and I thought to myself that this was the perfect occasion to take Kathy along on an impromptu European (working) vacation.

There was just one problem: Kathy didn't have a passport.

Of course, at the time I didn't recognize just what a significant problem this was. I was so naïve that I thought it would only be as difficult as making a trip to New York City.

Once we made it to the City, we went straight to the passport agency.

I should probably mention that it was Friday morning, the day we were supposed to leave.

There was a line two blocks long waiting to get into the passport office. Kathy was understandably nervous at the sight of it. "We're never going to make it."

I smiled. "Watch me." I had my uniform on and figured I could walk right up to the front of the line.

Unfortunately, there was a big NYC cop blocking my way. He puffed out his chest and pointedly read my name tag. "You any relation to Sean O'Holleran from the Bronx?"

Now, there are of course thousands of Hollerans and O'Hollerans scattered across this great land of ours, but this one was quick enough on his feet to seize a golden opportunity. "Not only am I Sean's kin, he sent me here directly to you to see if you could help us out."

The cop nodded. "Oh, he did, did he?"

"You see, I'm on duty and I'm being sent off to Germany tonight and I want my wife to come along with me, but she doesn't have a passport. I know that's a helluva problem, but Sean said there's only one man in all of New York who can fix us up."

"Me?" The cop smiled broadly.

I nodded. "You."

And just like that, the cop led Kathy and me to a special entrance to the passport office and put in a good word for us.

I know it sounds impossible, but Kathy was on the flight with me that night—new passport in hand.

And that wasn't the only time that being quick on my feet led Kathy and I into a wonderful adventure.

Towards the end of my active duty, there was a special Christmas gathering at the commanding general's home at Fort Monmouth. For us junior officers, the invites were allotted by lottery.

Let's just say that we were not among the lucky on that one.

Of course, luck has never stopped me from doing anything.

I had my dress blue uniform and the prettiest girl on the base (and in the world), and I was determined to go.

Kathy was nervous, but she looked lovely as usual.

She took my arm, and I walked straight into the event, the proudest officer there.

And no one noticed a thing. Or at least, no one said a word.

We had a wonderful time.

I have found that often the most important thing anyone can do in a situation is simply act like they belong there.

Oh, and smile. Always smile.

Chapter Twenty-Four

BEGIN AGAIN

When I first went off to serve my time on active duty with the Army, General Electric assured me that there would be a job waiting for me when I returned.

The "make good" on that promise was a position with the Military Defense Division in Syracuse, New York, where there was a facility that designed and built radars and sonars.

My job was manager of test engineering within the manufacturing department. It was, for me, something of a dream job.

Or at least it was a means of making a dream come true.

I was qualified for a GI mortgage, and with the new paycheck behind me, Kathy and I were able to sign the papers on a brand new Ryan Colonial. $23,500. It wasn't the biggest house on the block, but to Kathy and me it was like a castle. A castle of our own.

And castle was exactly what we needed, because while we'd been in New Jersey, Kathy and I welcomed our second child into the world—our daughter, Aileen.

And every princess needs a castle.

I was living my American dream.

Of course, every dream has its price tag, and mine was that new position.

I liked the work, but there were some minor troubles with a few of my coworkers.

Or rather, they had trouble with me.

There were essentially two teams at that facility: the design team, which created the concepts behind these state-of-the-art products, and my manufacturing testing team, which determined whether the design team's products actually worked.

It should have been an equal partnership, but the guys on the design side of the equation made a point of projecting an air of superiority over the rest of us. They were under the impression that they were better educated than us and that, because of their fancy diplomas, they were somehow entitled to be as condescending as they wanted to be.

The solution was a quick fix.

There was a Woolworth's at Fayette and South Salina Streets. They sold damn near everything, including picture frames. I went in one day and came out with a nice one, just like the ones that all of the guys in design had used to hang their diplomas.

The next day there was a meeting in my office, but the design guys were slow to start.

Their jaws were slack and their eyes were fixed on the new addition to the wall behind my desk.

"Something wrong, fellas?" I asked.

"I didn't know you had a master's degree," one of them said.

I casually turned over my shoulder as if I needed reminding, and then nodded with a smile. "Yup. NASA Fellowship."

"NASA Fellowship?"

I pointed back over my shoulder to my now-framed diploma. "I got my master's at the University of Delaware on a NASA Fellowship. I would've gotten my doctorate, but I got called up. Active duty. Army. You know how life is."

They all nodded.

After that, our meetings went much more smoothly, and no one talked down to anyone in my testing division any longer.

That did not, however, mean that everything went smoothly.

I remember the design guys once dumped a number of prototypes on us for analysis. These kinds of shenanigans were standard practice for them.

But this time, they put all that work on us late on a Friday afternoon, when they knew there was an important meeting the big kahunas scheduled for first thing Monday morning.

I guess their intention was to duck the results of their own work and make it seem to the big bosses as if my testing team was somehow behind in their work.

I smiled and wished everyone in the design division a good weekend as they filed out of the door a little early that afternoon, smug smiles on their faces.

As soon as they were gone, I went to my people and explained the situation. "How about we give them all a surprise? What if we all come in over the weekend and get the testing done.

That way, when we sit down on Monday, they'll be the ones left holding the bag."

I suppose there are some organizations where voluntary weekend work would have been laughed off, but not my team. Since my first day, I had gone out of my way to build relationships with each and every member, and by that point we were all more than willing to do whatever was necessary for one another.

> **Since my first day, I had gone out of my way to build relationships with each and every member, and by that point we were all more than willing to do whatever was necessary for one another.**

The entire testing division showed up that Saturday morning. They came back on Sunday, too.

We got the work done—and had more than a few laughs while we were at it.

When the meeting was convened that Monday morning, the design division guys shuffled in confidently and explained what they'd been up to, apologizing in advance that they wouldn't be able to discuss things further because testing division had yet to complete their work.

I smiled and tossed the reports on the middle of the conference table.

You could've heard a pin drop.

"We've done our job," I said. "When are you going to get us some more stuff to test?"

Chapter Twenty-Five

THE OPPORTUNITIES IN ANYTHING

Many people aspire to make a big impression with one fantastic demonstration or to establish themselves with a single, monumental achievement.

I'm sure this approach works for some people, but I've never personally seen it work out for the best.

Or at least it has never worked that way for me.

My time in Syracuse was one long day after another, and if it hadn't been for the joyous arrival of my youngest son, Brian, they all might have blurred together into one single slog through product trials and paperwork.

That may sound like a complaint, but I assure you it's anything but.

Every day was a challenge, and I was determined to turn that into my success.

Not necessarily anything that merited a memo to corporate headquarters, but a success just the same.

And those small achievements, day after day, were like bricks that I could stack together to build the foundation of a much larger structure.

Like a career.

Or a life.

So as the days in Syracuse passed from hot, humid summers to unbelievably snowy winters, I made the most out of every single opportunity that came across my desk.

And much sooner than I ever could have expected, what came across my desk was a promotion. Of sorts.

The position was with the GE Corporate Consulting Group in Bridgeport, Connecticut. The assignment was to evaluate each of GE's many facilities from an array of different perspectives in order to assess productivity and make suggestions for improvement.

Because of my background in manufacturing, I was asked to come aboard as the quality control guy.

I was thrilled by the opportunity.

Very few of my associates understood why.

I was thrilled by the opportunity. Very few of my associates understood why.

And their lack of enthusiasm for my new position wasn't completely lost on me. At a time when so many of the young Turks were climbing over one another to reach what they saw as "the Top," I understood that this seemed to many like something of a career detour.

It was, after all, an assignment to look at the work of others. I wasn't going to have the opportunity to make that career-making discovery or application that many of them were banking on.

And I was absolutely fine with that.

What other engineers saw as a dull bureaucratic assignment, I recognized as an incredible opportunity. It was a chance to see the company not just from the myopic perspective of a single office, but from dozens and dozens of different vantage points. Rather than focusing on just one part of a larger operation, I was being asked to take a look at the entire operation and figure out how it worked.

Any engineer worth their salt should've immediately recognized what an incredible opportunity that truly was.

And so I took to the road. And the skies.

> **Rather than focusing on just one part of a larger operation, I was being asked to take a look at the entire operation and figure out how it worked.**

I traveled all the time—across the Northeast, the South, the Midwest. I got to see General Electric up close, and I got to see America that way, too, and I learned a lot from both.

I learned a lot from my colleagues, as well. One of my favorites was the general manager, Al Taylor, who was as sharp a guy as I ever met. He was a prime example of what I meant when I talked about the "chemistry" between members of a team. From the first moment I met him, we shared a common understanding of our roles within the consulting group and, perhaps more importantly, the purpose of the group itself.

Very quickly, what might have been just another pointless foray into corporate bureaucracy gelled into a meaningful and productive means of evaluating operations and realizing significant improvements. What could have easily become a forgotten side project proved itself again and again as a real dynamo.

And the energy within the group was self-perpetuating.

Every new assignment fueled my imagination.

All the miles and all the months, all the individual pieces slowly but surely came together as an incredibly detailed portrait of the company in which I could recognize patterns that few others had the opportunity to see.

> **All the individual pieces slowly but surely came together as an incredibly detailed portrait of the company in which I could recognize patterns that few others had the opportunity to see.**

And one factor stuck out to me like a sore thumb.

We were traveling one day when I turned to Al and said, "Purchasing."

I think I might have woken him up. "What are you talking about?"

"Purchasing," I repeated. "We're going all over the place, looking the facilities over from top to bottom, and it's clear to me that our Achilles' heel is Purchasing."

If he'd been dozing off, he was suddenly wide awake. "How do you figure that?"

"Everywhere we've been, the personnel in Purchasing seem to be …" I was raised not to speak negatively about people, and I'd learned the practicality of following that sound advice in the corporate world, so I was hesitant to finish my thought aloud.

Fortunately, Al was willing to do it for me. "They're the B Team. Everyone knows that. Even the guys in Purchasing know that. All the guys who can't make it in Manufacturing or any other division all wash down into Purchasing. It's the company's catch basin."

"Exactly. But Purchasing is the start of everything. In fact, over 60 percent of the cost of running the General Electric Company is what we buy from other companies. It's the source of all the materials we incorporate into manufacturing. Everything else that happens is a ripple in the pond, but Purchasing is the pebble. And if they don't get it right, then those mistakes and missteps just keep multiplying and multiplying throughout the entire process."

Al looked at me, not like I was crazy, but like I'd just said something very important.

"You're saying that instead of making them the junior varsity, we should make them—"

"The pros. Absolutely."

He nodded. And smiled.

We took that small idea, that simple conversation over too many miles, and put our thoughts down on paper in a proposal. Before we knew it, our Corporate Consultancy Group had its own Purchasing Consultancy Group.

This wasn't a groundbreaking invention or earth-shattering innovation. It didn't change the company's street performance or make the shareholders stop and take notice. It wasn't any of the dramatic achievements that so many of my colleagues were waiting for.

But they were waiting.

I was *doing*.

And for me, that was a success.

Another brick.

Chapter Twenty-Six

MY GERMAN FRIEND

While I was with the consulting group, one of my assignments was to participate in GE's acquisition of Osram, a German manufacturer of lightbulbs.

And that meant going to Germany. A lot.

It also meant working with my counterpart at Osram. He was a nice enough fellow, older than me by at least fifteen years, maybe twenty. And quiet, seemingly immune to what I'd long considered to be my Irish-American charm.

We would have lunch together. And, if the work dragged on, sometimes dinner, too.

And sometimes we'd skip the meals and just sit with a couple mugs of beer.

Once in a while we would talk about his family or mine. Our project. The weather.

Mostly, however, we sat in silence with one another.

It wasn't an awkward silence between us, but the comforting kind, when you're appreciative of the company but grateful you don't have to say a word to keep it.

And then one evening, over a couple of steins, he did say a word. "Thanks."

"For what?"

"Your friendship."

I smiled. "Thank *you*."

He was silent for a minute. "It's odd that we should be friends."

"Is it?"

He nodded. "Life is filled with all sorts of unexpected things. Like our friendship."

I raised my mug. "Then here's to unexpected and wonderful things."

He clinked his mug to mine.

"I like you Americans." Then said, almost under his breath. "I didn't always."

World War II was raging when I was born, but even long after, I was certainly aware of some lingering aftershocks as I was growing up in Scranton.

In Germany, the effects were immediate and everywhere. Not distant whispers of the past, but inescapable reminders that their history was forever a part of their lives, present and future.

I was aware of the history, of course, but had never thought of raising it as a topic of our almost-nonexistent conversation.

"I want to tell you a story about the first time I ever met an American," he said.

It was odd to think of myself like that, as something he regarded as foreign.

"When I was fourteen, I was enlisted in the Hitler Youth." The words were clearly bitter to him and he washed them down with a long drink of his beer.

I could sense him searching my reaction for some note of judgment and condemnation, but I had none for him to find.

"I did not want to," he continued. "I was just a boy, not political. But there was no choice about anything in those terrible days." Another drink. "And when terrible days come, you'd be ashamed to discover what you will do just to survive."

He fell quiet, and for that brief moment I thought maybe that this was the entirety of what he wanted to tell me.

He took another drink, like he needed it.

"It was the end of the war. If there had ever been any point in the madness of it all, that time had long since passed. Everyone knew that it was a futile effort now—and that every life lost had been consumed by something wasteful and senseless."

I saw in his eyes that he had known more than a few of those who had been lost.

"The generals knew, but they didn't care. Generals never do. Why should they? They're not the ones who fight. Or die. So they took us, all of us just boys, most of them younger even than me, and they gave us the broom handles we used to train for marching maneuvers and they pointed to the western front and said, 'Go and fight.' But what they meant was 'Go and die.'

"One of the other boys was brave enough to ask, 'Why should we die for nothing?'

"'You don't die for nothing. You die to protect your mothers and sisters.'

"'Protect them from what?' we all asked.

"'The Americans,' they said.

"'The Americans?' Most of us had seen the movies. Cowboys. That's who we all thought would be coming. Roy Rogers.

"'No, no, no,' they all said. 'That's just make-believe. In real life, there is no greater monster than an American. They are coming towards us now, leaving nothing but carnage in their wake. And if you don't stop them, they will ravage your mothers and eat babies for breakfast.'

"'Eat?' We didn't know how this could be.

"'What do you think they are subsisting on?' they challenged us. 'They are an army of cannibals, viler than you could ever imagine, and if you don't protect your mothers and sisters …'

"And so off we marched, because boys believe what they are told. We all believed what we were told. And again there was no choice in the matter. No choice in anything.

"Three days later, we were close enough to the front line that we could hear the sounds of battle, the artillery. As we marched towards it, we were met by a group of soldiers. Germans, like us. But men, not boys.

"'Where are you going?' they asked.

"We told them that we were going to the front, that we had to protect our mothers and sisters.

"One of the soldiers looked at me and shook his head. 'Go home. Go home to your mothers and sisters.' I refused. I tried to push past him, but he shoved me to the ground and took my broom-rifle from me. Then he pulled me up by my collar, pointed me towards the east, and gave me a kick in the pants. 'I've seen too many boys die. I won't watch you die, too.'

"I tried to resist, but he was relentless. He pushed me all the way. All the way back to what he thought was safety. But it was back to Dresden."

He took a sip from his beer.

"That night there was bombing. The skies were filled with planes, and the night was filled with fire. The old soldier who was with me did not survive. I left him there among the debris and found a cellar, a hidden room, in a bombed-out building and huddled there, curled into a ball, certain I would be dead before the morning came.

"But the morning came, and I was alive to see it. But this, to me, was even more terrifying than the bombs that had fallen that night, because it meant that the cannibals were still coming.

"And then I heard the sounds of men. I couldn't tell whether they were Germans come to rescue me or Americans come to eat me. I was terrified, more terrified than when the bombs had dropped, because being eaten seemed a far worse fate than simply dying in a blast.

"There was a banging on the door. I tensed. The door came open, and to my great horror there stood an American soldier. I had nothing to fight him with and wouldn't have had the energy or aggressiveness even if I had a weapon. I was ready to surrender. To him. To my fate.

"That American—the first I had ever seen—looked at me, and the most curious thing happened. A single tear rolled from the corner of his eye, and then he came to me and pulled me to him in an embrace. He led me away from the rubble, and we found a house that was open. He took me inside. The woman of the house spoke a little English, and she told me that this American said I looked like his son. He gave her some money, and she gave me some milk and cheese. When you are hungry, I mean when you are

When you are really starving, the joy you find in a slice of cheese and glass of milk is a wonderful and unexpected thing.

really starving, the joy you find in a slice of cheese and glass of milk is a wonderful and unexpected thing.

"So, too, is the kindness of strangers. And the understanding that all men—except for the madmen and the generals—are all just looking to care for their loved ones and share with them some milk and cheese."

He looked at his mug. "Or beer."

I smiled.

"Friendship is an unexpected and wonderful thing," he said.

"It certainly is."

I've told that story a thousand times. Sometimes to make the point that there is always a perspective different from our own. Sometimes I offer it as an example of the universality of men, that despite the flags and banners, we are all really just trying to take care of the ones we love. And sometimes I tell it simply because it is a remarkable story of the human spirit, and I am forever grateful that this man—my friend—was generous enough to share it with me.

Despite the flags and banners, we are all really just trying to take care of the ones we love.

But whenever I tell it and whatever my motivations for the telling, I'm always sure to end it with that simple quote. "Friendship is an unexpected and wonderful thing."

Because it absolutely is.

Cherish the friends you have.

Work hard to make more, because you can never have enough.

Chapter Twenty-Seven

MR. HOLLERAN GOES TO WASHINGTON

Because I was concentrated on all the little things that too many others were more than willing to overlook and dedicated to doing the things that no one else wanted to do, I will never be sure what particular assignment it was that caught the attention of the corporate heads.

But something clearly did.

One morning, I got a call to come to my boss's office.

"Marty, have you ever heard of the President's Executive Interchange Program?"

I admitted that I hadn't.

"Have you ever heard of the White House Fellows?"

I had.

"Well, it's a lot like them, except they actually do stuff."

He went on to explain that during the Johnson administration there had been an initiative to foster economic development by taking thirty-some promising politicos from within the executive branch and exchanging them with an equal number of businessmen from the private sector who had demonstrated the ability to rise to high management positions, placing them in government positions which offered significant challenge, responsibility, and regular and continuing contact with senior officials. That was the President's Executive Exchange Program.

I appreciated the civics lesson but wasn't sure why it had been shared with me, until he clasped his hands together and said, "Marty, General Electric has decided that we'd like you to be our representative in the program. Would you be interested?"

What was there to say? Would I like to be the GE delegate to go to Washington and work in the president's program? I can't even say that I thought that one over.

"Yes. Yes, I would."

I was so excited that I'm not even sure that I talked the offer over with Kathy, which I always did. I suppose I must have known her reaction to the opportunity, which included a corresponding program that incorporated the participant's significant others into meetings and activities of their own.

By this time the Holleran family was like a military unit, able to tear down, mobilize, and reestablish a base at a moment's notice.

In any event, by this time the Holleran family was like a military unit, able to tear down, mobilize, and reestablish a base at a moment's notice. Before we knew it, we had moved from Bethel, Connecticut, into a house in Reston, Virginia, and been absorbed up into the "Beltway life."

There were a number of opportunities across a wide array of agencies that were available to me. I interviewed with a number of them, but found myself once again following my gut to the position that felt right for me. There might very well have been one position or another that suited my resume or career ambitions better, but I found myself drawn to take a position within the Department of Agriculture at the Farmer's Home Administration (FmHA).

The FmHA is a financial institution that makes loans aimed at developing the agricultural community. Not many people have heard of it—I hadn't before I became involved in the interview process—but at the time, it was one of the largest banks in the United States, managing funds well in excess of $30 billion.

I understand that the idea of an electrical engineer with General Electric suddenly working for a bank that makes home and farm loans to rural Americans might appear nonsensical on paper, but in the real world it proved to be a perfect match.

I learned a lot about the banking industry, and our country, too. But most of all I forged some important personal friendships, particularly with retired Brigadier General Frank B. Elliott, USAF, who was assistant secretary to the Department of Agriculture and headed the FmHA.

My arrival with the FmHA coincided with the conclusion of a protracted piece of litigation in which the FmHA had been embroiled. A number of the little hometown banks that dotted the Midwest and rural South had sued the FmHA, alleging that the loans offered to farmers effectively deprived the small banks of the interest they may have generated on those loans. When I first learned of the case it seemed a ridiculous theory to assert, but one of my first assignments was to handle the resolution of the matter.

A settlement was reached in the amount of $15 million, and that amount was divided among the assorted plaintiffs. Dozens of checks were written for the interest allegedly lost by the litigious banks. Some were only a couple of thousand dollars, but a number were for far more significant amounts. My responsibility, as a representative of the FmHA, was to deliver each of the checks—by hand, one by one.

And so I spent a fair portion of my first weeks in Washington far outside of the Beltway, actually traveling the country, checks in hand.

Like many of the other assignments I'd pulled in my corporate career, I was keenly aware that some might have viewed the task as something beneath my rank (which, by the way, was a GS-16, the civilian equivalent of a general or admiral), but I relished the opportunities it encompassed.

Even with all the traveling I'd done with GE, I got to see a lot of America that I had previously overlooked.

By that time, a collective mindset had already formed that regarded America as a collection of cities with God-knows-what filling in all the miles between. Although my time with GE's consulting group had broadened my horizons, I confess to having failed to fully appreciate the vastness and complexities of rural America. Forsaking the usual jet that soared overhead and bypassed the heart of the country, I traveled on the asphalt that crossed the country, and the process was like discovering my own country for the first time—meeting people, understanding their different ways of life.

A fascinating experience.

When the conversation turns to travel, people often ask me which country I've enjoyed discovering the most. My answer is always America.

Chapter Twenty-Eight

THE EVER-DWINDLING BREAKFAST GROUP

I arrived in Washington during the summer of 1976. A presidential election year that saw incumbent Gerald Ford running against a candidate that few on either side of the aisle were taking seriously, a former governor who'd been reduced in most press coverage to "that peanut farmer from Georgia." Jimmy Carter.

Although the President's Executive Interchange Program was essentially nonpartisan, I had nevertheless entered the program under the Ford administration and was surrounded by his political appointees, including General Elliott, who was a terrific boss to work for and an even better friend.

The general taught me everything I needed to know about the high art of finance and running a bank.

But most of all, he gave me a master's course on politics. And people.

There was a tradition in place that summer that a good number of the bureaucrats and politicos would gather together in the mornings before starting work to share a cup of coffee, a bite of breakfast, and a bit of conversation about what was happening within the Beltway. And at that particular time, this meant they discussed the upcoming election.

Most of all, he gave me a master's course on politics. And people.

When I started in July, President Ford was comfortably ahead in the polls against "that peanut farmer from Georgia." Every morning, the collection of bureaucrats and career government types gathered to share their political insights on how Ford might deliver the *coup de grace* and what they might all likely expect from him in his second term.

Those breakfasts had been crowded affairs.

And then, as the humid summer began to give way to lower autumn temperatures and the leaves slipped from the trees, President Ford's place in the polls began to fall, too.

One morning after this slight turn of fortunes, General Elliott took me aside and quietly shared with me, "Take a look at who's here right now." I scanned the room and took note of our usual coffee companions. "If the president continues to fall in the polls next week, you take another look around and see how many of this bunch is missing."

Seven days later the president's number had dropped again, and when I looked around our group, I did notice that we were missing one or two of the original members.

The general whispered to me. "If it gets worse next week, there will be even fewer."

Sure enough, the president's lead in the polls continued to erode, and with it I began to notice a corresponding erosion of our breakfast group.

"What's happening?" I asked the general.

"They're all career bureaucrats, here at the behest of the Republican president. And now they're covering their bases. Some don't want to be seen with this group and associated with the Republicans. Others are jumping off this possibly sinking boat and trying to find a position in the private sector before the other rats beat them to it."

"But their positions here?"

"Are just that, positions here. Let this be a lesson to you. For the most part, people's loyalty follows their self-interest. That's not a bad thing or a good thing. It just is. But it's an important thing to always keep in the back of your mind."

By the time the election came around, our numbers had thinned to a skeletal crew.

And on the morning after they announced that "the peanut farmer" had done the impossible and won the White House, the general leaned over to me and said with a smile, "Just you and me."

Lesson learned.

Chapter Twenty-Nine
"THEY'RE NOT LISTENING TO YOU, DAD!"

One of the truly amazing functions of our system of democracy is that it was created specifically with a mechanism to accommodate for and facilitate a peaceful and (relatively) seamless transition from one presidential administration to another. And so when Jimmy Carter won the election that November, everyone in the Department of Agriculture who had served under Ford realized that it was time to turn in their resignations.

They all did.

Including the general.

Everyone … except me, the President's Executive Interchange Program guy.

The transitional protocols are a shining example of democracy in motion, but they aren't perfect—or very functional.

And so by January, when Jimmy Carter was sworn in as the thirty-ninth president of the United States of America, there weren't any Ford appointees left at Agriculture. None.

And of course President Carter, who had just taken office, had yet to appoint their replacements or have them confirmed.

The transitional protocols are a shining example of democracy in motion, but they aren't perfect—or very functional.

As a result, for that time between the departure of Ford's people and the arrival of Carter's appointments—for that one brief window in history that our Founding Fathers certainly never could have anticipated—I was the acting administrator to the Department of Agriculture and the (unlikely) temporary head of the Farmers Home Administration.

Of course, the business of government goes on in spite of all this, and the new year meant that a new budget needed to be presented to Congress. Without anyone else to make that presentation, it fell to me to testify before a Congressional committee.

I had anticipated many things when I first came to D.C., but testifying before Congress had not been among them.

I had anticipated many things when I first came to D.C., but testifying before Congress had not been among them.

As an electrical engineer from GE, I suppose I should have been nervous (even terrified) by the prospect of making such an appearance and giving testimony on the proposed budget of a federal bank with many billions of dollars in assets. I understand that I probably should have been, but I never had a moment's doubt.

This wasn't because I had any sort of faith in myself as a master of finance. That wasn't the case. What put my mind at ease and what I relied on 100 percent was the people surrounding me.

The bureaucrats at the Department who were there on a nine-to-five grind and not on a political whim really stepped up to support me. These were my kind of people. Roll-up-your-sleeves-and-get-to-work people. And when we were done with our work, I might have been the most thoroughly prepared witness to ever get sworn in before a congressional committee. In that regard, I cannot fully express my appreciation for the professionalism of the FmHA federal employees.

I owed a great deal of gratitude to the Congressional staffers, too. I think they sensed the earnestness with which I approached my testimony and respected the reverence I held for the institution. They walked me through every step of the process so that when it was finally my time to appear, there was nothing to it.

There was nothing to it, but the event meant the world to me personally.

That this kid from Prospect Avenue in the South Side of Scranton was appearing before Congress was an occasion that stirred a myriad of emotions within me. And it was one that I wanted to share with those who were closest to me.

Kathy was there, of course, along with my mother-in-law, Anna Jordan, and my son, Marty, all in their Sunday (or Congressional) best.

And for all that happened on what was for me a historic day, my favorite memory is of my son Marty. He was old enough to stand his own ground but not yet mature enough to understand how business gets done in D.C. So while I was reading my opening remarks into the record, he took particular offense at some congressmen who were privately discussing another matter amongst themselves.

"Dad, they're not even paying attention to you!" he blurted out.

His comments demanding respect for his old man were actually recorded into the Congressional Record. And to this day, I smile—and am immensely proud—that there is not one, but two of the Holleran men whose comments are preserved for all time in the annals of American history.

Chapter Thirty

JUDÍAS VERDES

There were many amazing experiences incorporated into my year with President's Executive Interchange Program, but one of my most memorable—and certainly Kathy's favorite—was a two-week tour of Europe. It was a once-in-a-lifetime opportunity to travel across the Continent with stops not only in every major political and cultural center, but ornate parties and dinners and special celebrations at a jaw-dropping selection of embassies and palaces and mansions—a taste of Grace Kelly and Cary Grant's Europe.

Obviously, Paris was a much-anticipated destination. We landed at de Gaulle and were immediately whisked off to a restaurant that even the snobbiest Parisians regarded as fancy.

Magnificent place.

We landed at de Gaulle and were immediately whisked off to a restaurant that even the snobbiest Parisians regarded as fancy.

Keep in mind, with thirty from government and thirty from business, together with significant others, we were a party of one hundred twenty.

And at this event there was a French contingent that was nearly the same size.

Now with so many bureaucrats and executives, there were more than a few of our group who were used to being in the spotlight and enjoyed being there. I'll freely admit to being one of them.

Still, when we arrived in the City of Lights, there was one American who clearly viewed the occasion as his solo opportunity to shine. He made a point of flaunting the fact that he was bilingual, and for some reason everything he had to say in French was much, much louder than anything he'd ever said in English.

We were all seated in this incredible dining room. Crystal chandeliers and murals on the domed ceiling, crystal and silver on the table.

As soon as the last of us had taken our seats, the wait staff began to take our orders, no easy task.

When the waiter came to this man's wife, she, like so many of the rest of us, began to point at her menu while good-naturedly trying to sound out the pronunciation of what she was hoping against hope might be a tasty meal. No sooner did she start this process when her husband completely shut her down, shooting her a look like she'd just been caught putting the silver in her purse. He snatched the menu from her, and in a volume the whole place couldn't help but hear, he proceeded to order dinner for her. "*Judías Verdes!*"

He snatched the menu from her, and in a volume the whole place couldn't help but hear, he proceeded to order dinner for her. "*Judías Verdes!*"

As soon as he was done ordering for his wife, this show-off bounced up out of his chair and rushed to the dais to introduce the speaker who'd been asked to speak to our group. He made the introduction in French, of course, and then paused to wait for applause that never came.

I didn't understand a single word, but I recognized that he'd said something that was off-putting to our French hosts.

I leaned over to the gentleman seated next to me and asked him what had just happened.

In a discrete whisper, he explained that the show-off from our party must have intended to say to the speaker, "Your audience is waiting for you!" Instead, however, he'd made a slight, but significant error and said, "Your audience was waiting for you."

The distinction was a minor one, but the native French speakers had taken the introduction as an insult, meaning that the audience had once wanted to hear from him, but were no longer interested.

I smiled.

The show-off came back and sat down next to his wife, unsure what had gone so subtly-but-oh-so-noticeably wrong.

At that same moment, the waiter returned with the special order the man had put in for his wife. "*Judías Verdes!*" the server said proudly and set down the biggest plate of green beans I have ever seen in my life. That's it. Just green beans. Nothing else. A heaping helping of green beans piled on an enormous platter.

Mrs. Show-off gave her man a look that didn't need any translation.

There's a time to step out into the light for your solo and a time to be content to be a part of the chorus.

That was a time to sing harmony. Everyone knew it but that one guy.

The bonus lesson here is that on those occasions when one forces their solo, you have to be absolutely certain that you can steal the show. And then do it.

The guy had tried to be Maurice Chevalier and came off like Pepe Le Pew.

And just like that, all of his personal capital was spent for the remainder of the trip.

Chapter Thirty-One

CALCULATING THE AIRSPEED VELOCITY OF AN UNLADEN SPARROW

Even in a city like Rome, where every time you turned your head you saw something even more beautiful than what you'd just been looking at, the American Embassy and its surrounding grounds were achingly beautiful.

There was an outdoor reception in the main garden, and the just-setting sun cast a golden hue over everything. It was one of those cinematic settings captured in ethereal light.

Our group was scattered across the lawn. I was standing, sharing a conversation and a drink with the Italian ambassador. It was a perfect moment.

But life is rarely perfect, and at just that particular instant, a bird was flying overhead, and it let loose with a dropping that plummeted earthward and landed dead center in my Scotch, splashing the amber goodness all over the sleeve of my suit.

> **It let loose with a dropping that plummeted earthward and landed dead center in my Scotch.**

The ambassador was embarrassed, as if he'd somehow been responsible for the incident.

The people surrounding us were all aghast.

And me?

I just laughed it off.

Of all the stories I have to tell, this certainly isn't the one that means the most to me personally, but it was one I wanted to be sure to share, because I think there's a very important lesson to be learned in it.

I've got a master's degree in electrical engineering.

I survived Father McGee's remedial math.

I can work numbers.

But even I can't imagine how you would begin to calculate the odds of that bird taking flight at just the right moment to be positioned overhead so that the released "payload" would fall directly into the glass of Scotch I just happened to be holding down below. Who could begin to work out the probability of a situation like that occurring? Or take anticipatory measures to prevent it?

> **Sometimes shit is just going to drop into your life.**

And that's exactly my point.

Sometimes shit is just going to drop into your life.

It's going to happen.

And there is absolutely no point in wasting your time trying to figure out how it happened. Or (even worse) why it happened.

It's simply going to happen.

To all of us.

Over and over again.

And when it does, the only option any of us have is to determine what our reaction will be. You can become embarrassed and slink away from the party. You can make a big deal about it all and shake your fist at the sky, cursing that cruel, mocking bird.

Or you can just have a good laugh and get yourself a new glass of Scotch.

Take it from me, that's the way to handle it.

Shit happens. Don't take it—or yourself—too seriously.

Have a laugh, share a story, and get a clean glass of Scotch.

Chapter Thirty-Two

THE MOST BEAUTIFUL GIRL IN THE WORLD

What I remember most about that reception in Rome is not the bird or the Scotch or the collection of international business and political dynamos who were there that evening. What I remember most is the sunset.

And her.

With fresh drink in hand, I continued making the rounds of the party, talking for a moment with this corporate wunderkind and sharing a story with that parliamentarian. It was quite an experience. Dignitaries and European counterparts. Celebrities and the full assortment of beautiful people.

The sun was just beginning to set. The sky was streaked with reds and yellows and oranges like a Renaissance landscape.

I just happened to turn, and there across the crowd I caught sight of Kathy, doing what she always did ... being wonderful.

And I'm telling you, in that moment, my love for her hit me like a physical thing.

> **There across the crowd I caught sight of Kathy, doing what she always did ... being wonderful.**

Kathy had married me when she had no real reason to. She's taken all of those words that fit so easily into the lyrics of silly love songs and made them real, and she's lived them every single day we've been together. She's demonstrated her love for and faith in me by accompanying me on the craziest adventure two kids from Scranton have ever taken.

We moved about like corporate gypsies, but she never once objected or complained. Instead, she made certain that we always had a home, no matter where we went.

When this assignment or that held me at the office late into the evening, there was never anything waiting for me when I returned home except a dinner plate in the oven and an even warmer embrace. When I was called upon to travel, no matter how long the trip's duration, there was always a bit of "home" packed in my bag and a bright *Welcome Back!* to celebrate my return.

And most of all, she was a better mother than any man could hope to have for his children. Marty, Aileen, and Brian never had the advantage of stability in attending the same school year after year, but Kathy made certain that there was a rock-solid foundation for them at home, and from that grounding she raised them to become the truly remarkable adults they are today.

During our tour of Europe and probably over the course of my career, Kathy was too often dismissed as Marty Holleran's wife. Not that there's anything derogatory in that identification. Not at all. But I'm afraid it fails to acknowledge what a remarkable woman she is in her own right and what an essential component she was in every single part of my life.

Everything I've written here is true, but there are no words truer than this: I could not have done any of the things I've done in my life without my wife, Kathy. None of it.

And so while I have an entire book of advice about how to live a wonderful and meaningful life, my most important bit of wisdom is this: wait for the person you love and who loves you back.

Don't rush it.

Don't compromise.

It is a decision that is all too easy to make for all the wrong reasons, but it is undoubtedly the most important decision you will ever make.

In the exact moment that I looked across the crowd of reception guests and found her there, Kathy must've sensed my gaze, because she turned to me and offered me a little twinkle of a smile. Just a little sign of the connection between us.

And I knew then what I've always known: that whatever happened in my career, in my life, I had already achieved the only success that really matters in this world.

And in a room full of royalty and rulers, I knew for certain that I was truly the richest man in the place.

Chapter Thirty-Three

BREAKFAST WITH A CHAMPION

I won't lie, leaving D.C. behind and settling back into the life we'd been living before that whirlwind experience was a challenging adjustment.

Kathy made it easily.

And the kids did their part, too.

And so before the autumn leaves had begun to fall from the oaks in our front yard, life had returned to normal for the Hollerans—or at least as normal as it got for us.

And normal felt good.

But it didn't last.

I was just wrapping up the last of a long work week when the phone on my desk rang. It was an unexpected invitation to breakfast. From Jack Welch.

Jack Welch is a legendary executive now, but at the time he was senior vice president in charge of Engineering Plastics. He was a dynamo, developing new products and companies and spinning them off. And he was doing a terrific job.

Reginald H. Jones was Chairman and CEO of GE at the time, but everyone knew that change was in the air. There were maybe four individuals who were mentioned in discussions about who might take over the reins from Mr. Jones, but Jack was far and away everybody's heavy favorite.

I flew to Pittsfield, checked into the Hilton where Jack had his offices, and prepared for a breakfast meeting about I-didn't-know-what.

In the morning, I went down to the hotel restaurant where I was scheduled to meet Jack.

Jack's head of HR was there, but no Jack.

The HR guy and I knew one another informally, and we talked for a minute or two.

And then waited.

And waited.

No Jack.

The restaurant was crowded that morning, and in addition to those already seated, there were maybe twenty of us, men and women in business suits, all waiting patiently on the other side of a string of velvet ropes for an open seat.

All of a sudden, a jolt of personal energy hit the hotel lobby like a tornado tearing across a prairie cornfield. It was Jack Welch.

He walked like he was late. Or rather, like he didn't have a single second to waste.

All of a sudden, a jolt of personal energy hit the hotel lobby like a tornado tearing across a prairie cornfield.

"Marty," he called out like he knew me better than I did. "Jack Welch."

When I was just a boy, my father once told me, "When you shake a man's hand, give him a firm grip and look him straight in the eye."

Jack's father must've had the same conversation with him.

"Let's get a seat," Jack said, and then, ignoring the velvet rope and the others waiting behind it, he headed straight into the dining room.

I followed him, sheepishly pushing past the others.

None of them said a word.

When we were seated, Jack snatched up the menu, looked it over, and put it down just as quickly. He wasn't a guy to debate the options; he made decisions. Even when it came to breakfast.

"Marty, I heard you've done some great things in D.C."

I realized that this was the introduction to my interview, and I took a deep breath, readying myself to deliver the pitch I'd prepared.

Jack didn't have time for that.

He turned to the head of HR. "Listen, we know we're going to hire him, so let's just find him the position that suits him best and get him started."

And that was that.

There was no interview.

Not even a job offer, really.

There was just a decision.

And that was just Jack Welch.

Chapter Thirty-Four

JUST JACK

It turned out that the position that was the best fit for me was as a project manager at Engineering Plastics.

And it was a perfect fit. I loved it.

And I excelled at it.

So much so, that I wasn't there for more than a year before I was offered a significant promotion. General manager of a department. It was the realization of a dream I had been chasing after for a long time. Responsibility for a P&L business, including manufacturing, engineering, finance, marketing, and sales.

El jefe.

Les capitan.

The boss.

I was going to be the captain of my own ship, and the thought of assuming that command was more than exciting.

I should've known better.

I was winding things down with my old position. The promotion had come up out of nowhere, so there was a very quick transition that had to be made. It was a Thursday night, and I was due to start this new adventure Monday morning.

The phone rang. It was Jack Welch, who had moved to GE headquarters to run the consumer sector.

"Marty, how are you?"

I'd quite naturally assumed that he'd called to congratulate me on the new promotion, and I was about to tell him just how over-the-moon fantastic I actually was, but he cut me off.

Jack didn't have much time for pleasantries. There was work to be done.

"I need you to come down to Fairfield," he said.

The request was so casual and offhand that the purpose of it completely escaped me.

My confusion was real. "For what?"

His seemed equally perplexed. "For what? I've got a job for you."

The answer only heightened my level of confusion. "Job? Jack, I just got a new job.

General manager. I start Monday."

"Forget about that," he said, like the realization of my dream was nothing for me to be concerned about.

"I don't want to forget about it, Jack. It's everything I wanted. It's—"

"Listen, Marty. I need you down here. We're growing businesses. Starting new ventures. I need you down here."

"Jack, I'm flattered, but I really don't want to go back to a staff position, now that I've earned—"

It was then that Jack made it clear that he'd already made his decision—and that his was the only decision that mattered. "Marty,

I need you here with me. I want you to become one of my project managers."

And that, as they say, was that. I just said, "Yes sir."

Someone else took that general manager job I'd worked so hard to get.

I moved to Fairfield and got to work for Jack Welch as one of his project managers.

Wasn't I disappointed? At first, perhaps. (And by "perhaps," I mean "a lot.")

But I was quick to dismiss that disappointment. I had a job to do and I got busy doing it.

And in the end—as is so often the case—that initial bit of dissatisfaction was completely unfounded. Good things happen, even when we don't recognize them at the time. As it turned out, going to work for Jack Welch was one of the greatest strokes of good fortune to ever befall me in an already blessed career.

I've always trusted my instincts, but I've also learned to trust that everything will work out in the end. I've had as many disappointments and "failures" as the next guy (maybe more), but I've never focused on them or let them deter me. Instead, I've always made the effort to seek out the opportunities and advantages in my situation.

That's not always an easy thing to do, but it's a skill worth mastering.

> I've had as many disappointments and "failures" as the next guy (maybe more), but I've never focused on them or let them deter me.

Chapter Thirty-Five

THE KID IS ALL RIGHT

Another job meant house hunting, which by this time Kathy had perfected to a process that she executed with all of the precision and momentum of a Special Forces operation.

Sometimes these migrations brought us back to a place we'd been before.

It was the sort of warm summer day that teases you with just a hint of the cooler breezes to the north but still carries all the humidity of the city. We already knew the neighborhood, and Kathy was running her expert examination of one of the dozen or so listings we'd lined up for that day, and I was taking a break out front, watching the kids.

Across the street and down the block, there was a small group of boys playing. Harmless games, but the volume and tone of their voices identified them as "the kids" of the neighborhood.

Aileen and Brian ignored them, but Marty's ears pricked right up.

His back stiffened, and he said to me, "Dad, I'll be right back."

Then, without another word, he started right for the boys.

I didn't know the boys, but I had an idea who (or what) they might be.

While he had been in school before we'd started our stint in D.C., Marty had had a few brushes with a bully, and I knew that these incursions had troubled him.

He'd asked me for advice, and I'd told him the only thing I could: a bully is a bully, and you either have to face them or you have to learn to live with them—and facing them, as tough as that is, is a helluva lot easier than living with them.

A bully is a bully, and you either have to face them or you have to learn to live with them.

He marched right up to the boys. "My name is Marty Holleran."

The boys stopped whatever game had demanded the top of their voices and fell silent.

The clear leader of the pack stood up.

Marty had grown quite a bit since their last encounter, and it seemed as if the boy didn't recognize him.

"I used to go to school here," Marty said.

The kid shifted in his Converse.

My son said, "You used to bully me."

Much hemming and hawing and claims that everything had all been a joke. The usual bully backtrack.

"I just wanted to let you know that you won't be bullying me this year," Marty said.

No one appeared to have any problem with that.

Point made. Marty turned around and walked right back to us.

When you're a parent, you worry about your kids. All the time. It's just part of the job description.

But every once in a while you get some small confirmation that your kid is going to be all right.

Marty took a seat next to me without saying a word about what had just happened.

He didn't need to.

In that silent moment, I knew the kid was going to be all right. And I know he did, too.

Chapter Thirty-Six

A VERY BIG STICK. AND A GOOD-SIZED CARROT, TOO

Working for Jack Welch was a master class in business.

And psychology.

Much has been written about him and his managerial style, but every single word of it needs to be considered and weighed in light of the monumental challenge he'd been presented with. When Jack assumed the role of Chairman and CEO, General Electric was over a hundred years old, and its policies, protocols, and general outlook were every bit as conservative as that might suggest. He was tasked with dragging one of the largest and most established corporations in the world into not just the latter half of the twentieth century, but into the twenty-first century as well.

No easy task.

That required shaking things up.

Including sometimes people.

On one occasion, I was part of a senior team accompanying Jack to Louisville, Kentucky, to review a manufacturing facility we had there. The Big Boss's arrival was a momentous occasion in Louisville, and they really put on a show for us. Lots of razzle and dazzle.

One of the featured performers was the chief legal counsel who handled the company's legal matters. He was a gentleman of fifty or so, old enough to merit respect but not yet to the point of seniority that might leave him susceptible to the charge of younger bulls. He was invulnerable in his environs and held himself with the air of someone who was used to being respected and deferred to, distinguished in a very Southern way.

He rose to his feet, straightened the line of his tailored suit, and announced in his best courtroom-thespian voice, "I'm quite proud to say that in all of the years that we have been managing the legal affairs here in Louisville, your business here has not had a single lawsuit. Not one." He puffed out his chest just a little bit more.

Looking around the room, I could see that most everyone was impressed by that announcement. Lots of head nodding and smiles.

There was one exception.

Jack Welch was *not* impressed. Not in the least. "What did you just say?"

The room went as quiet as a morgue.

The lawyer cleared his throat and tugged at his collar. "I said that in the entire time we've managed the legal affairs, we have not defended a single—"

"I heard what you said." Jack's tone was sharp.

If at all possible, the room got even quieter.

"You're a consumer business!" Jack shouted. "You should have a lot of lawsuits! You should be pushing the envelope down here. And when you push the envelope, you get sued.

That's how business gets done."

The now-flustered lawyer wanted to frame an eloquent excuse, but all he could put together was a string of "but-but-buts."

Jack didn't have time for that, either. "Get him out of here."

I'm quite sure Jack was the first person who had ever spoken to that Southern gentleman in quite that way, but thirty seconds later the lawyer was gone.

Now, it's possible that someone might have come away from that event (or a retelling of it) with the impression that Jack had been unnecessarily hard on the man. I suppose that's up for everyone to decide for themselves.

I can tell you with all certainty, however, that no one else in that room ever thought complacency was the secret to success at GE ever again.

To light a fire under a company, sometimes you need to strike a spark.

And sometimes that has to come off the seat of someone's pants. That's just how it is.

I learned a lot about the value of a little shock therapy to

> **No one else in that room ever thought complacency was the secret to success at GE ever again.**

get the entire organization moving. Jack Welch wielded a very big stick.

But he was also generous with the carrots, as well.

He was fiercely loyal to "his people," including me. If you had proven that you were deserving of his confidence, then he was more than willing to extend you the independence to handle your own assignments in your own way—even if that meant, from time to time, that you fell short of your goals.

Working for Jack Welch was a challenge, and the key to meeting it was to never settle for complacency, to constantly push that envelope. And in that way, Jack always got the best out of his people. He certainly got the best out of me.

Chapter Thirty-Seven

THE GREAT LAS VEGAS AIR CONDITIONER LASER AND LIGHT SHOW

A short while after I accompanied Jack Welch to Louisville, I had the great pleasure of returning to the Derby City to take a position at that same GE facility—general manager of Marketing and Sales.

My domain: window air conditioning units.

Now, believe it or not, major appliances and consumer electronics has always been something of a sexy industry. And at that particular time, technology had thrown open the door to a whole new world.

Televisions were bigger, thinner, brighter, and louder. VCRs revolutionized how we watched them. High fidelity had turned the corner with the advent of the CD, and stereo systems had developed the capability to recreate studio sound in the consumer's home. Microwave ovens were all the rage. Answering machines. Portable music players. It all may seem trite by today's standards, but at the time home electronics brought us the first tempting taste of The Future that had been promised to us in so many sci-fi movies and Saturday morning cartoons.

And then there were window air conditioning units.

They weren't new, and they hadn't evolved into anything space-age. They hadn't changed much at all since they'd emerged on the market in 1971. They simply did what they'd always done: they kept the temperature cooler inside than it was outside. That's it.

And that was the problem with window air conditioning units.

People will comment all the time about how sharp the picture is on that state-of-the-art TV or how great their favorite song sounds on that gotta-get-it stereo. Pieces like that practically sell themselves. But absolutely no one takes any notice of a window air conditioning unit (until, of course, the mercury climbs, but that's another matter).

In a sexy industry, they are decidedly unsexy.

Now, every year there is a Consumer Electronics Show in Las Vegas. It's a big thing. For that industry, it's like the Super Bowl, the Oscars, and the World's Fair all rolled up into one big ball and dropped in the center of the glitter capitol of the world.

The TV people bring their biggest, newest sets and play specially created programs to show off the colors and sharpness of their screens. Show attendees stand there for hours, mesmerized by the scenes of swimming tropical fish or hot air balloon races. "*Oooooooh!*"

The stereo guys show up and set up displays that have speakers on top of speakers on top of speakers. They put on the top hits of the day and turn the volume to 11 for crowds of convention-goers who dance in the aisles. "*Wow!*"

And then there were window air conditioning units.

How do you show off one of those units in a convention hall that's already over-air conditioned? Flapping blue strips of paper taped to the vents?

Decidedly unsexy.

Or at least that was what the conventional wisdom and a long history of previous exhibits would have had you believe.

At the time, I had a young guy in my marketing department named Larry Johnston. (Yes, *that* Larry Johnston, but this was long before he was the Larry Johnston of Albertsons fame.) He had taken it upon himself to come up with an exhibit for the Vegas show that would blow the doors off of all the home appliance, TV, and stereo guys. And one day he brought that idea to my office.

"Lasers!"

I was not overly receptive. "What do you mean lasers?"

"Lasers," he explained. "It's amplified light that's focused through—"

"I have a master's in electrical engineering. I know what a laser is. What's less clear is what that has to do with air conditioners."

"We're going to use them in our exhibit in Vegas."

It wasn't the craziest idea I had ever heard, but it was certainly in the photo finish. "What are you talking about?"

"Our exhibit. In Vegas. When people stop by our booth this year, we're going to give them a laser show. *Zap! Zap! Buzz!*" He acted out the extravaganza he pictured in his head.

> It wasn't the craziest idea I had ever heard, but it was certainly in the photo finish.

If nothing else, his enthusiasm had caught my attention.

We talked. Brainstormed. Exchanged ideas.

When we were done, we had designed the most kick-ass laser light show Vegas had ever seen, and in the center of it all was the sexiest star of them all: window air conditioners.

Now, here are two things to keep in mind if a similar desire to put on a laser show should ever strike:

The first is that everything about lasers requires absolute precision. (Thus the phrase "laser-like precision.") If the timing of our show was off by the slightest fraction of a second, if we positioned the necessary equipment slightly askew one way or another, if there was any deviation at all from the plan we had drafted—the entire show would be a huge flop and a sales failure.

Which brings up the second point: Laser shows are ridiculously expensive.

We got the money we needed from the bosses, but Larry and I rolled into Vegas like two high stakes gamblers, knowing that absolutely everything we had was riding on that laser display. The importance of the annual show and the budgetary commitment I had made to our laser display made the demonstration a "make it or break it" event. If something went wrong and we failed to bring our vision to life, it was unlikely there would be any corporate forgiveness. There certainly wouldn't have been any understanding about why a missed opportunity had cost so damn much money.

Our careers were on the line.

But sometimes life requires you to put everything out there and spin the fortune wheel.

Sometimes standing pat is the worst gamble you can take. The secret is to remove as much of the unknown from the equation as you possibly can.

The secret is to remove as much of the unknown from the equation as you possibly can.

By the time Larry and I got to Vegas, we had done all of our homework, and then some.

We knew exactly how the display was going to be set up. We'd walked through the show a thousand times. We came equipped with extra bulbs and cords. Every possible situation had been considered, every angle had been covered.

And that's why when I finally pushed that button for the first time, it wasn't so much like spinning the roulette wheel as it was unleashing a whole-lotta-awesome.

Lights flashed and strobed, lasers shot out and danced all across our exhibit—just exactly as we'd planned.

People stood, awestruck. Crowds gathered. Word spread. Crowds grew.

Who had time for fish on TVs or Top 40 hits at earsplitting levels? The air conditioner guys had lasers.

Lasers!

We had taken a risk and created a spectacle. And it had paid off spectacularly.

And that was the year that the sexiest thing in Las Vegas was window air conditioning units.

Chapter Thirty-Eight

TWO WORLDS

Eshajori is a Japanese word that roughly translates to "People meet, always part."

It's used to express the temporary and transitory nature of all human relationships, and certainly that would apply to my career.

I accepted every assignment with the unspoken understanding that it would only be for a period of time—some longer than others, but most not long at all—and then I would be off somewhere else, doing something else with someone else.

Working under Jack Welch was a pleasure and an honor. The position, at the pointy end of the power pyramid of a Fortune 10 company, represented a level of achievement I didn't even know enough to aspire to when I first started with General Electric. It was challenging and demanding, and it made me a better executive. And I'd like to think a better person, too.

But I always knew—in the back of my mind, at least—that it was temporary, too.

In 1985, GE bought RCA for a cool $6.28 billion. Corporate pocket change.

I think the primary objective in the acquisition was to acquire NBC and enter the broadcasting arena, but RCA—forever associated with the iconic image of Nipper the dog listening in bewilderment to his master's voice over a Victrola—had a substantial consumer electronics business as well.

When the acquisition happened, I was elected a GE corporate officer and given the job of overseeing the Sales and Distribution divisions of both companies.

Even the most benevolent corporate acquisition is not unlike a military takeover. New leaders, new policies and procedures. And because of this, the employees of the acquired enterprise are always understandably nervous about what they can't help but regard as an uncertain future.

They also can't help but regard the employees—particularly the managers—of the acquiring company as agents of the Dark Side. They're either too bitter or too wary to cooperate much. It's understandable. They're afraid they may be sealing their corporately mandated doom, or they're overly solicitous to prove their worth and extend their tenure so they can continue paying their mortgage and feeding their family.

Addressing the RCA employees for the first time, I was keenly aware of their concern about what the acquisition meant to their individual futures and their prospects for continuing as a team.

At the same time, I also knew that I was being evaluated as well.

Asserting my will too aggressively would be just as ineffective as failing to make clear that changes had been made—and there was a new sheriff in town.

All of these considerations, normal in any acquisition, were only made more complicated by the fact that you could hardly have found two corporate cultures that were more dissimilar—almost polar opposites. As I've said before, GE was synonymous with the white-shirt-black-tie conservativeness of the post-World War II Golden Age of Eisenhower economics, while RCA was ... let's settle on *less conservative.*

> **You could hardly have found two corporate cultures that were more dissimilar.**

And this already volatile situation was further complicated by the fact that at this particular time, RCA was first in consumer electronics and GE was a distant third.

Merging these two businesses into a single, efficient unit required very special handling. The secret is working together as a team, and the "chemistry" of that team is everything.

Now, I have known some really smart people, folks for whom genius would not be a compliment but a simple statement of fact, and I've worked with some folks who possessed really special talents. But for all the personal qualifications, if people can't get along with one another and play their respective part on a much larger team, then their individual abilities never offset the liabilities created by that personal failing.

On the other hand, if you've got a true team together, everyone understands their role, and there is uniform commitment to fulfilling those plans and facilitating their coworkers, then there's nothing that can't be achieved.

Before I'd even gotten started, I knew that putting two different cultures together is difficult at best. So what I decided to do from the very beginning was to make sure I had a good blend of both RCA and GE management on my team, even though I thought at the time that the GE executives were better as individual performers. I knew that after a period of time, whatever factors distinguished one group from the other would dissipate and the best performers would excel, while those who couldn't contribute to the team would expose themselves and be replaced.

And so I took some of the top guys I knew from GE, but I didn't load my team up with them. Instead, I got to know the people from RCA just as well, and I chose the best of them all.

Between those two hiring pools, I put together a team that understood the Herculean task we had ahead of us and was committed not only to getting that job done but also to exceeding whatever expectations had been put on us by our corporate higher-ups.

I knew I could count on the GE people from the get-go, but I was surprised by how quickly the former RCA employees responded to my managerial approach. The vast majority of them had expected nothing more than a pink slip, and when they found themselves rewarded with a previously unknown level of autonomy and individual responsibility, they really shined.

I knew exactly how I wanted the business to operate, and I gathered them all together for my obligatory pep talk. Instead of the sermon of damnation that is too often preached on these occasions, I made my expectations clear and my faith in them all even clearer. And I left them all with this mission statement: "Let's make this business dance!"

And that's exactly what we did.

There's a (natural?) tendency in business—and in life in general—for some people to micromanage the hell out of everything. It's a serious mistake. Business (and life) is not a solo sport. It requires a team.

And so the most important thing any manager can do is put aside concerns of which individual can do what and concentrate instead on building a team that incorporates and maximizes the strengths of all while compensating for their shortcomings as well.

Business (and life) is not a solo sport. It requires a team.

Resumes are all fine and good, but the most important quality of a new hire can't be found on a sheet of paper. The deciding factor should always be whether they have *It*, that know-it-when-you-see-it certain something, that personal chemistry.

Chemistry is everything.

Chapter Thirty-Nine

CHIPPER

W.C. Fields once famously observed, "Never work with children or animals."

I wish I'd paid closer attention to his advice.

Technological advancements had made it a particularly exciting time to be involved in the consumer electronics market. On one hand, there had been an unparalleled explosion of new products on the market, and everyone wanted a piece of this brave new world. CD players. VCRs. Answering machines. Projection TVs.

On the other hand, improved technology had significantly reduced manufacturing costs, which thinned the profit margins where a number of new entrants in the game had significantly tightened competition.

And all of this was further complicated by the fact that for the first time since the end of World War II, the majority of consumers no longer placed a premium on buying products from companies based in the United States. To the contrary, the foreign competition was all too often perceived as cutting edge, sleeker, and more stylish.

So at a time when consumers were drawn to all things modern, I was stuck with a corporate symbol of a dog listening to his master's voice coming from the horn on an Edison-Bell cylinder phonograph.

At a time when consumers were drawn to all things modern, I was stuck with a corporate symbol of a dog listening to his master's voice coming from the horn on an Edison-Bell cylinder phonograph.

Nipper, the dog confused by the fidelity of those newfangled sound-making machines, had been the original mascot of Gramophone's Victor record label since 1900 and had been transferred to the Radio Corporation of America when they purchased Victor in 1929.

And to give the little devil his due, that faithful pup had been (and continues to be) one of the most recognized product mascots in the world. But the world had changed significantly since he'd made his debut, and the image of a dog and a Victrola did absolutely nothing to sell high fidelity stereo equipment. Or anything else.

And so, what to do?

We had a product mascot that was so beloved it had become incorporated into the American zeitgeist, but no longer drove consumers to the point of purchase and failed to convey the message needed to market our products moving into the future.

We couldn't just Old Yeller the lil' guy.

And yet, we couldn't go on with him, either.

The answer was obvious, or at least it should've been. In truth, it may have taken the marketing people a moment or two before someone asked, "What's the one thing that absolutely everybody loves?"

The answer, of course …

Puppies!

Nipper would have a puppy, a young, energetic counterpart that could lead RCA into the modern age.

Anyone who has ever gotten a puppy knows that more than vet shots or housebreaking plans, there is one decision that is more important than any other: the name.

There were dozens of suggestions thrown out, but the best one of all was "Why don't we hold a contest and let the public name him?"

And that was exactly what we did.

Naming a corporate puppy seemed like a cute way to promote the brand, but I can't say that any of us foresaw what that would become.

In a pre-Internet day when "viral" was still a bad thing, the Name the RCA Puppy contest absolutely blew up all across the nation. There was coast-to-coast coverage from newspapers and magazines, including, unlikely enough, *Playboy*, which featured an interview with me about the promotion. (I swear I only read it for the article about me.)

In a pre-Internet day when "viral" was still a bad thing, the Name the RCA Puppy contest absolutely blew up all across the nation.

The national interest was so fevered that when it finally came time to announce the contest-winning name, *The Today Show* booked us to do it live on their program.

So, one New York morning, I found myself in the NBC studios with Bryant and Katie, Al and the gang. I was dressed out in my best suit, all made up, and impeccably groomed.

Somewhere between the morning news and the celebrity du jour, the slot for our segment came up and I was escorted to a couch. Once seated, one of our marketing guys came along and presented me with the cutest mixed-terrier pup anyone had ever seen. A furry white ball of adorableness.

We went live, and the interview began.

My little doggy-buddy sat in my lap as I discussed RCA's movement into the future and our quest to represent that modernization with the addition of a new canine mascot.

"So, does he have a name?"

I smiled. "After reviewing hundreds of thousands of entries in our contest, we have settled on a name for this little guy. America, let me introduce you to ... Chipper."

There was collective *"Awwwwwwww!"* heard across America, echoing from Portland, Maine, to Portland, Oregon.

Chipper cocked his little head, as cute as can be.

And then, on live TV, RCA's new mascot peed right in my lap.

I should've listened to W.C.

Chapter Forty

MY BIG BROTHER, JACK

This is a beautiful life, but I can't say I've always understood it.

I had an older brother. His name was Jack.

Jack was a year older than me on the calendar, but he was not a particularly good student—which is a loving brother's way of saying that he was a terrible student—and so somewhere along the painful path of Catholic school, the two of us wound up in the same grade.

Like twins.

Except that Jack and I were very different from one another.

While I went to extreme measures to gain entrance into the University of Scranton, Jack couldn't get out of academia quickly enough, and as soon as he was reluctantly handed his diploma, he was off.

What he never found in school, Jack discovered in the U.S. Air Force. The regimentation and tradition brought out something in him that the nuns never could, and he distinguished himself in his service.

With the Cold War heating up with every passing day, America was quick to flex its military muscles with a show of force along Europe's eastern borders, and Jack was one of those airmen who were sent to an air base in Germany.

He wasn't stationed there all that long before he wrote home with news that he had met the perfect woman. Her name was Gail, a lovely young woman with a remarkable ability to put together those final few pieces of Jack that even the Air Force couldn't quite fit. She completed him.

They got married.

And within a year or two, they were parents.

A son, John.

Then a daughter, Lynn.

The kids meant everything to Jack.

The Air Force brought the young family back to Texas. Jack was happy enough, but Gail quickly realized what he was too comfortable to ignore: that the restrictions that the military placed on a man without a college education would put corresponding limitations on their lives.

She decided that there was something Jack needed to do for himself, and for his family. So, Jack went back to school.

I'm certain Jack never would've done it for himself.

And I don't want to speculate, but going back to school—the institution that had always heightened his personal sense of inadequacy—was such a daunting prospect to him that I'm not certain he would have enrolled just to satisfy his spouse, no matter how much he loved her.

But there was nothing he wouldn't do for his kids. Nothing.

Jack enrolled in college there in Texas, and to everyone's surprise—most especially his own—he not only survived academia, he absolutely excelled. He rose to the top of his class and graduated *magna cum laude.*

And that led to Officer Candidate School, in which he finished first in his class.

My big brother, Jack. The Air Force officer.

After a long and distinguished military career, Jack retired from the Air Force and started a consulting company which promised to provide all of those extra material comforts that he and his family had sacrificed in the service of their country.

My big brother, Jack. The Air Force officer.

Life was perfect.

Until suddenly—in a single instant—it wasn't.

Jack's daughter was just a teen, but she had been on that same route a thousand times before.

This time, however, she shared it with a careless driver who was so distracted by something other than the road that they never even noticed the car Lynn was riding in.

The accident was cataclysmic.

The injuries Lynn suffered were so terrible that the grim-faced doctors all told Jack there was nothing they could do—his daughter had lapsed into a coma, and she was unlikely to ever emerge from its confines.

My big brother, Jack, told all those doctors that they were wrong. He told every last one of them that his daughter would not only survive, but that she would walk out of their hospital. He promised them all that she would rise above her injuries and go back to the life she'd led before.

Even if Jack didn't have a plan for how he was going to make all that happen, he was determined to make every word a reality by sheer force of will.

So for weeks Jack stayed by his daughter's bedside in that hospital.

He never left her.

He worked there in her room—he set up an office for his burgeoning consulting practice and conducted "business as usual" right next to the machines keeping his little girl alive.

He took his meals there.

On the rare occasions when his body broke down and insisted, he slept there.

Mostly, he prayed there.

He prayed and prayed.

We all did.

And then contrary to the predictions of those medical naysayers (or maybe just realists) who had all written Lynn off as a patient without a future—she opened her eyes.

It was a Christmas miracle.

We were all grateful, but no one could have been more overjoyed by her reawakening than Jack.

And then, everything he had put into maintaining her vigil, he dedicated toward seeing her through the long, hard road to rehabilitation.

He stayed by her side when she needed him.

He worked her through all those excruciating physical therapy exercises, hurting more than she did with every painful repetition.

He did everything she needed, including taking her to rehab.

Religiously.

He drove her into town so that the physical therapists could do for her what he couldn't.

The roads were rain-soaked that day. If it had been some other occasion or destination, Jack might very well have stayed home until the weather improved, but Lynn had a rehab appointment and he was determined that she was going to keep it.

Jack was going to do whatever his daughter needed him to do. No matter what.

So on that miserable day, Jack and Lynn set off down the highway like it was any other trip to the rehab center.

Jack was driving cautiously for the perilous conditions, but he didn't take any special notice that a couple car-lengths ahead of them there was a car with a mattress strapped to the roof.

And he never saw the moment that those tethers fell slack and the mattress slipped loose, tumbling off onto the rain soaked pavement.

Just ahead of Jack's car there was a truck that ran over the mattress and dragged it for a bit. The heat from the truck's undercarriage set the mattress on fire just as it fell beneath the wheels, which acted like a pitching machine and shot the flaming mattress back out and onto the hood and windshield of Jack's car.

He swerved, but couldn't fully avoid the mattress.

His car skidded on the slick asphalt, but Jack wasn't one to panic. Ever.

One man in a million could've avoided a horrendous wreck, but Jack was just that man.

Jack wasn't one to panic. Ever.

He managed to stay in control of his vehicle under those outrageous circumstances and was able to pull the car safely to the side of the road.

It was a miraculous maneuver, but Jack had already proved himself a master of miracles.

And after all, he was carrying precious cargo. Lynn.

She was his only thought at a time when any other man might've completely lost their composure.

Jack was a military man. So once he made sure that there was nothing wrong with his daughter besides being understandably shaken by the incident, his mind moved next to securing the scene and making sure she was safe within their vulnerable position at the side of the road.

He got out of his car to see what could be done to make certain that their stopped car was not in jeopardy from oncoming traffic, but in the midst of that rush of cars was some thoughtless SOB going more than seventy miles an hour over those rain soaked lanes.

No one knows whether or not he even saw Jack, but it doesn't really matter.

The SOB was going too fast to have ever stopped in time.

My big brother, Jack, was airlifted to the hospital, but he'd used up all of his miracles on saving his daughter. He died two days later.

This is a beautiful life, but I can't say I've always understood it.

I miss my big brother, Jack.

Every damn day.

Chapter Forty-One
KINTSUGI

There is an ancient Japanese practice of repairing shattered ceramics and porcelain with a gold seam between the fractured pieces. The philosophy behind the custom is that bringing together the various shards with a precious metal makes the piece more valuable than it had been in its original, unbroken state.

I'm not sure about cups and pottery, but that's certainly true in business.

My efforts to integrate GE and RCA's consumer electronics divisions went smoother than anyone could've possibly hoped for.

I had gone out of my way not to play favorites with any of them and had intentionally staffed our twelve sales regions with six managers that had come over from GE and six that had been at RCA. I knew that any other division of authority—say, one favoring the people I knew from GE—would have completely demoralized those who had remained from RCA.

I put them all in the mix and then stepped back to let things work themselves out, confident that the cream would rise to the top, as it almost always does.

In a year's time I had built a team that operated with more cohesiveness than similar units I had worked with that had members who had all come up through the same corporate developmental system. Here I had a group of people who understood what I expected from them and knew that I respected every one of them enough to allow them the freedom and leeway necessary to accomplish that—and more.

I was grateful to have fostered such unity in my division, because since the very first day I'd taken over the show, I'd known there was a monumental task ahead of us that could only be accomplished if we all worked together.

At the time of the acquisition, GE had been shipping their consumer electronics directly to retailers. RCA, however, had clung to an outdated chain in which they dealt with independent distributors who in turn supplied retailers.

It was an unnecessary extra step—and a fairly costly one at that. What the distributors made on the transactions had to be added to the cost of the goods and then passed on to individual consumers. That meant higher prices, and that was killing RCA's sales across the board.

From the day I signed on, I was aware that these independent distributors were going to have to go, but I knew the process wouldn't be a simple one. Business is business, but it's conducted by people, and those people form relationships, often very strong ones.

Those district managers who had come over from RCA

> Business is business, but it's conducted by people, and those people form relationships, often very strong ones.

had known the distributors in their districts over a long time. They were friends. They were a comfortable part of the "old way" of doing business. And I knew that if I moved to remove them as soon as I took my seat behind the big desk, I would lose the confidence of all of those loyal RCA people. I didn't want to begin on that note.

Instead, I waited.

A year later my team was united in purpose, and whether they had come from GE or RCA was completely irrelevant to me, to the rest of the team, and to themselves. I had earned their loyalty.

And when the time was right, I called a meeting and sat everyone down, explaining that the current market simply wouldn't allow for the markups created by utilizing independent distributors.

Everyone understood. And agreed.

Everyone was on board, and the transition went off with a military precision.

Patience and loyalty had earned me their respect and loyalty.

It was a perfect equation, and the product was significantly increased numbers on our bottom line.

Chapter Forty-Two

THE FATHER. THE MOTHER. AND THE HOLY GHOST.

Over the course of my life, I've enjoyed a number of positions that were both incalculably challenging and extremely rewarding.

None of them was ever a patch on my role as a father.

From the first time I held my first-born son, I was keenly aware of the responsibility I bore, not just to my children but to the rest of the world as well. It wasn't enough to just protect and provide for mine (although that was certainly always at the top of my personal to-do list); it was simultaneously incumbent upon Kathy and me to transform these little bundles of joy that we both thought were the greatest kids that had ever graced the planet into the sort of adults that would make this world a better place, too.

I always knew that this same objective posed certain struggles for my parents, who had limited resources to provide for my brothers and me, but there were equal challenges for Kathy and me, who had worked so hard to secure for our family those extra comforts that we had never known in our own childhoods.

There was one particular teenaged conversation. I don't remember the subject or even which child we had it with, because after a while they all tend to blur into one another. But whoever it was hit me with the now familiar refrain "So you think it's easier for me just because I grew up with the things that you didn't?"

I took a deep breath. (I highly recommend this tactic to any parent of a teenager.) And then I said as calmly as I could, "No. Just the opposite. I think the privileges that your mom and I have worked so hard to provide you with have only made it harder for you."

I took a deep breath. (I highly recommend this tactic to any parent of a teenager.)

Someone's eyes got bigger at my unexpected response. "What do you mean?"

"I mean, your mother and I started with next to nothing. When we left for Delaware to start our life together, we didn't have anything more than the cash in the wedding envelopes."

An exaggerated teenaged sigh.

"But this is your baseline." I gestured around the comfortable setting that was a whole world away from the public housing accommodations I'd known at Hilltop Manor. "Everything that you have to build starts from here. Getting here was hard enough, believe me. But taking it up to the next level … no, that will be much, much harder."

I don't think there was any adolescent reply other than a silent realization of the enormity of the implications in what I'd just said.

And that really was the extent of whatever teenage rebellion we had with the kids.

I think our secret to the relative serenity of our home life was the gypsy lifestyle we necessarily adopted as a result of the corporate transfers and promotions that defined my career. That external chaos necessitated a certain domestic tranquility.

Over the years, Kathy and the kids moved with me a total of fifteen times.

That averaged out to about a new house every year.

New schools, too.

New friends.

New everything.

> **Over the years, Kathy and the kids moved with me a total of fifteen times.**

That's not a lifestyle I can prescribe to anyone else. I've certainly heard tales of others in similar situations who found themselves torn apart by the frequent relocations, but I think for the Hollerans it melded us into an even stronger family unit. I think that was especially true for the kids, who forged an unusually strong bond among themselves in confronting the shared challenges of moving so often.

And it forced all three of them to become more self-reliant and independent.

They would, from time to time, complain about the demands that our situation placed on them, and I would let them know, "You have to be able to take care of yourself, because there's not always someone else to do things for you. It's just your mother and me and the Holy Ghost, so you better learn to do it for yourself."

And that's exactly what all three of them did.

In his senior year of high school, Brian was given the honor of addressing the assembled guests before graduation. The topic that the school had assigned him for his address was "The time I felt closest to God."

Brian never once asked me for help with his speech or gave a practice run of it to Kathy.

So it was a complete surprise when Brian strode across the stage, adjusted the microphone at the podium, and began, "St. Agnes Elementary, 1974. Reston Elementary, 1975. St. Mary's, 1976." Brian went on to list every school he'd ever attended.

In order.

There were a lot of them.

When he was done, Brian said, clearly but softly, "I'm Brian Holleran. My parents moved twelve times and I've gone to twelve different schools. Each time, my mom and dad would walk me into the school and introduce me to the principal, and then the principal would walk me down a hall to another new classroom and introduce me to my class. I'd go to whatever desk was empty and take my seat. And that's when I felt closest to God."

Without a word, he collected his pages and walked off of the stage.

The place erupted in applause.

I clapped along, too, but it wasn't just his speech I was applauding. He had been given a difficult path to walk as a boy, but it had made him a man centered in those same fundamentals that have guided me throughout my life.

When we were done with our ovation, Kathy took my hand and squeezed it once. I looked at her and knew exactly what she was saying without a single word.

Parenting is the toughest job anyone can ever have, but if you do it right, the rewards are so much greater than you could ever hope for. It has defined my life.

Chapter Forty-Three

I NEVER LEARNED THE WORDS TO *LA MARSEILLAISE*

France.

The sights are breathtaking.

The food is wonderful.

And the only thing more complicated than the bureaucracy of their government is the bureaucracy of their business—so imagine the result when the two are intermingled.

In 1982, then-President François Mitterrand nationalized two electronics concerns, Thomson-Brandt and Thomson-CSF. Sometime after, Thomson-Brandt and Thomson-CSF were merged to form Thomson Consumer Electronics.

None of this would have posed any more than a passing interest to me except that among Thomson Consumer Electronics's various concerns was a medical business that GE was interested in purchasing. Talks commenced, and when the deal makers were done, GE had acquired that medical business in exchange for transferring to Thomson the rights to make and sell RCA- and GE-branded televisions and other consumer electronics products.

Sometime after this, the French changed the name of Thomson Consumer Electronics to Thomson, *Société Anonyme,* or Thomson SA for short (no, I don't know why).

It shouldn't come as any surprise that I was assigned the task of making sure that the marketing, sales, and distribution transition went as smoothly as possible.

Still, it's necessary to stress that this was not merely a French company, it was a company *owned* by the French. They did things in their own way.

I found this out very early in my tenure.

Shortly after my arrival, I received a furious fax from the company's chief financial officer. The communiqué contained a charge that the numbers I had reported were completely off and that this was setting the stage for disaster within the company.

There was only one problem: My numbers were accurate; it was his calculations that were wrong.

I suppose the French have a way of handling situations like this. Diplomacy. Discretion.

But I'm just a guy from the South Side of Scranton, and I have a way of handling things, too.

I told my secretary to get the CFO on the phone.

A moment later, I had the number three guy in the company on the line. Although there was 3,500 miles and a good-sized ocean between us, I could tell from the silence on the other end of the call that he was more than a little taken aback by my call.

What he didn't know was that it was about to get much, much worse.

I told him my figures were right.

He protested.

I told him his figures were wrong. Even louder.

And that's when I completely lost my patience.

"Look," I said, cutting him off. "The numbers you're throwing around here are wrong and I can prove it."

I'm not entirely sure what the guy's play was—whether he was really so stupid that he couldn't read his own numbers or whether he was trying to run some second-rate intimidation game on me, thinking I'd cower and be his pawn for the duration of my tenure.

Whatever his angle, he'd picked the wrong guy.

It's not often you hear a Frenchman stammer, but that guy couldn't get the words out. He said something about it all being a simple mistake and then something else about his interpretation of the numbers being his opinion.

I wasn't having any of it. "Pierre," I told him. "Everyone has a right to their opinion, but nobody has a right to be wrong in their facts! You're trying to bully me here, and I won't stand for it. I won't. So I tell you what I'm going to do, I'm going to go straight to the Chairman and I'm going to tell him that whether you're a bully or a moron, I won't work with either one. And then I'm going to get you fired. What's your opinion about that?"

He didn't have so much an opinion as a flurry of pleas to my kinder, gentler, and more forgiving nature.

Whether it was the schoolyard or a boardroom, I've just never been able to countenance a bully. That's especially true when it has to do with someone besmirching my reputation.

The name Holleran means something to me. A lot.

Whether it's in business or life, your reputation is the *you* the world meets whenever you're not around.

"I'll tell you what I want," I said.

> **Whether it was the schoolyard or a boardroom, I've just never been able to countenance a bully.**

He fell quiet as soon as he realized we were negotiating and there might be a way out for him.

"I want a letter of apology," I said.

He fell silent.

The French certainly have their own way of dealing with things, but from his response I gathered that didn't include demanding written apologies from corporate officers.

I didn't care. Not one bit.

And twenty minutes later, the very same fax machine that had brought the aggravation into my life groaned and clicked away again.

I kept that letter of apology in my desk drawer for the entire time I was there.

And that turned out to be longer than I had first expected.

At least, longer than the first two CEOs I served under for five years.

And they were good guys. Both of them. We accomplished a lot in those five years, and it was a real pleasure working for them.

The third gentlemen to take the helm of Thomson SA, however, was something else altogether.

He was a French bureaucrat running a nationalized business.

I was an American businessman trying to grow a business.

Somewhere in between those two positions, between those two men, there was a serious disconnect.

There was no blame involved, no fault.

There was just no chemistry between us. And as I've always said, "If the chemistry doesn't work, then nothing works."

I knew from the very first time that I met him that it wasn't going to work out.

I also knew it was time to look for the next opportunity.

Chapter Forty-Four

THE LONG AND (NOT SO) LONELY NIGHT, PART II

Back when I was studying the Classics at the University of Scranton, I came across the work of Ovid, who told the famous tale of Midas, the Phrygian king who was granted what he most wanted … and starved to death as a result.

When my time at Thomson SA had come to its amicable but inescapable conclusion, I considered returning to General Electric. There were a number of positions that I could have walked right into.

But after close to thirty years, that was the primary drawback for me. I didn't want a job I knew I could do. I wanted a challenge.

More than that, I wanted to run the show. My way.

And not just any company.

> I didn't want a job I knew I could do. I wanted a challenge.

I was looking for something traded on the NYSE.

Something in the field of consumer electronics.

It was a long list of wants.

And that's why when a finance group approached me with a dream position that checked every single box, I couldn't help but think it was the answer to all my prayers.

It turned out to be something much different.

Oh, at first it was exactly what I had hoped it would be: an entire operation that was mine, to be groomed and grown in accordance with my philosophies and the lessons I'd learned.

> **At first it was exactly what I had hoped it would be: an entire operation that was mine, to be groomed and grown in accordance with my philosophies and the lessons I'd learned.**

And for the first few weeks, I saw those plans coming together and caught a glimpse of the future I knew we could build.

And that's when everything changed.

Nothing major. Not at first.

There were little things. Whispers and rumblings.

The kicker came when I realized that the man who had organized the investors and hired me in the first place had plans of his own.

There was never any plan to bring the company back to its former glory. To the contrary, the plan was to accelerate its demise. There wasn't a goal of making a profit, there was only an intention to drive the enterprise into bankruptcy, sell it off in pieces, and buy back the valuable components for dimes on the dollar.

There was nothing wrong with that plan.

Nothing illegal, at least.

It was a common practice of the day and I'm confident that I could have continued to play along and that I would have profited handsomely from the arrangement.

But there was something morally repugnant in the deceitful transaction that I could not countenance.

> There was something morally repugnant in the deceitful transaction that I could not countenance.

Maybe even more important to me, however, was that I couldn't stand being lied to or used in that fashion. There wasn't any future payday that would have made that arrangement something I could live with.

And so that brings us back to exactly where we started, with me standing with that resignation letter at the fax machine.

A once-in-a-lifetime chance ready to be thrown away forever.

And now you're wondering: Did you do it? Did you fax the letter?

You bet I did.

I faxed that letter, went back to that opulent office, and packed up everything that was mine. It only filled a single box.

I drove home and told Kathy what I'd done.

I suppose some other wife might have been furious about the money I'd left on the table or complained about not having been involved in the decision. But my wife, my Kathy, came to me and put her arms around me. She looked up at me with those eyes I've never tired of looking into and said, "If you think that's the right thing to do."

"It was. It was the right thing. That's why I had to do it."

She smiled and hugged me. "Then I'm with you. Always."

And she always has been.

Chapter Forty-Five

WHAT REALLY MATTERS

Over the course of my career, I achieved a level of success that I'm quite sure I didn't even know enough to aspire to when I first joined General Electric: the President's Executive Interchange Program, working for Jack Welch, my position overseeing the RCA acquisition. They were all rewarding endeavors, but each carried its own challenges, and all were demanding of my time and attention.

Travel was a frequent requirement, and when I wasn't on the road, late nights and early mornings were understood to be a necessary part of the job. Seven days a week. It was a difficult schedule, to be sure, but I was able to survive those demands because I approached them with my personal priorities very much in place.

No matter how far this position or that took me from my boyhood streets of South Scranton, I never forgot the advice my father offered me about planning my life not around my dreams, but on the foundation of something that would mean far, far more: my family.

There were times of professional triumphs and darker periods when it seemed like this project or that was destined for failure, but there was never a day that passed without me remembering my father and his sage advice—and being eternally grateful for them both.

I'd achieved far more than my parents could've hoped for me. Or Father McGee could've expected of me. I had even earned the respect of Jack Welch.

But my true success was and always has been my family.

For whatever I was able to offer them in terms of consumer comforts, my family had to make significant sacrifices. Kathy would no sooner have turned our latest house into a home when there was another moving van pulling up to the curb and the process started all over again.

New house. New community. New friends.

For our kids, it meant one new school after another and all of the pressures and demands that this nomadic existence places on any kid who's trying to find their special place in this world.

For our kids, it meant one new school after another and all of the pressures and demands that this nomadic existence places on any kid who's trying to find their special place in this world. The friends and achievements at one school were left behind as they had to start from scratch in the next. These were circumstances that would've tried and tested any young adult, but each and every one of our children excelled under these extraordinary conditions.

And we excelled as a family together.

And while I am—by my very nature—reluctant to take credit for much, I will tell you that I played no small part in our success as a family. With my father's advice echoing always in my ears, I made certain that no matter how jammed my work calendar was, it never took precedence over my personal schedule.

No matter what job title I held, I made sure that Kathy and the kids knew that I was always a husband and a father first.

I made Little League games and school plays whether that meant leaving the office a little early to make the twenty-minute drive or whether that necessitated taking a transatlantic red-eye from Paris to make that first pitch or opening curtain.

> I made certain that no matter how jammed my work calendar was, it never took precedence over my personal schedule.

And I never regretted a single mile of it.

I truly believe that to achieve ultimate professional success, one must find a motivation greater than simply a career. My family has always provided me with the much-needed motivation to do all of the little things, all of the impossibly hard things that combined to make my career the triumph I always felt it was.

Every minute I was pulled away from the four of them, I was focused on providing them the very best that I could. And every minute I was fortunate enough to get to spend with them, I was conscious to savor it all, knowing that life is too fragile to take even a minute for granted.

Family is and always will mean everything to me.

And that is what made what happened so terribly devastating.

Chapter Forty-Six

A HOSTAGE TO THE WORLD.

Growing up in an Irish Catholic community in Scranton in the 1960s, it seemed like every house had the same two oil paintings on the parlor wall.

One was a portrait of Irish Jesus, looking wistfully off into the heavenly horizon.

The other was JFK. Smiling.

I've always admired President Kennedy. Whatever the political takeaway from his years in office, I doubt this country has ever had a more philosophical leader, and his eloquent observations have often resonated with me—none more so than when he paraphrased Sir Francis Bacon and said, "To have a child is to give fate a hostage."

Having children is like having cataracts removed from your eyes: in a single instant, everything is suddenly brighter and clearer than you ever could have imagined before.

The wonderful.

And the horrible.

It's sincerely not my intention to diminish the experience of anyone, but having children represents a complete paradigm shift that one can never really prepare for and once experienced can never really articulate fully.

> **Having children represents a complete paradigm shift that one can never really prepare for.**

The closest I can come to any suitable explanation now is that before I became a father, I never really knew what love was. Or joy.

And I had no real concept of regret. Or fear.

I have always been well aware of and grateful for the blessings that have been bestowed on me throughout my life, but at the same time and by my own reckoning, I am no stranger to tragedy, either. Adversity and I are old friends.

And that's fine.

A long time ago, I made my peace with adversity and accepted it as just another inescapable component of this life; something to be managed, but not feared.

But that was for me.

That was my personal philosophy for those times when life singled me out to visit its indiscriminate cruelty upon.

Me.

I was less prepared when it was my children who found themselves in fate's icy cold grip.

And I was completely unprepared when the victims of tragedy were my children's children.

What can I say about my daughter, Aileen?

Every father wants to be "the man" in his little girl's life, but she has always been, and to this day remains, one of my greatest heroes.

At this particular time, she was just starting her life, really.

And it was a perfect life.

Her husband, John Crowley, was a handsome midshipman from the U.S. Naval Academy. Georgetown. Notre Dame Law School. Harvard MBA. Everything a young woman could want in a partner (and everything her father could want for his daughter).

Aileen and John had a son, John Jr.

When John was in his last year at Harvard, they let us know that they were expecting their second child. A daughter.

They named the little girl Megan. She was the answer to a thousand prayers and a perfect little angel to her parents. And her grandparents.

Yet almost from the beginning we were all silently aware that there was something to be concerned about with this precious little one. Kathy would hold her granddaughter and then whisper to me with barely constrained panic that there was something about the baby that didn't feel right in her arms, that she wasn't developing the way any of us hoped.

The situation with Megan was trying, but just after they moved to California, our concerns were temporarily distracted by the arrival of Aileen and John's third child, a son they named Patrick.

Neither the joy nor the distraction lasted long.

Soon after Patrick was born, Aileen and John realized that they needed some help for Megan. They were desperate for a diagnosis, a name for the unidentified affliction that was now clearly affecting poor Megan. This began a tour of doctors, specialists in this field and specialists in that. None of them seemed to make any headway towards being able to put a name on what was wrong.

Kathy had gone out to California, I think partly so that she could help Aileen with the grandkids and partly because she couldn't stand to be away from her own.

John called me one afternoon. His voice was soft and sad. I had never heard that tone before. "Dad. You need to come out here. Now."

I don't remember much after I hung up.

The room may or may not have spun around me in vicious circles as I struggled to process the news. I probably cried, but I'm not certain. I don't remember much more.

> **The room may or may not have spun around me in vicious circles as I struggled to process the news.**

I've spent a lot of time on a lot of airplanes in my life. I'm certain that I must have logged a million miles in the air, but none of them passed as agonizingly slowly as the ones separating me from my family on that particular day.

I sat in my seat and watched the country pass beneath me, achingly slow.

There were four hundred million people down there. And at the time, I couldn't believe that any of them could even imagine the sorrow I was feeling.

Chapter Forty-Seven

STRENGTH TO GET THROUGH THE NIGHT

The oversimplified explanation I was given to understand a very complex situation was that Pompe disease was an inherited condition that inhibited the body's process for managing the cellular storage of glycogen, a complex sugar, in various organs and the muscles. As a result of this uncontrolled buildup of glycogen, the affected organs broke down and the muscles failed to develop normally. Eventually, the condition simply overwhelmed the afflicted.

The disease was untreatable.

The mortality rate was 100 percent, with sufferers given only a matter of months to live after the diagnosis was made.

I had never heard of Pompe disease before that harsh introduction, and there was every good reason for that.

The condition was so incredibly rare that at the time it was thought that only one out of forty thousand children born has this condition—fewer than a few thousand worldwide. It turns out that both John and Aileen were recessive (or silent) carriers for this disease. Even then, there was only a one in four chance that any of their children would have it. After Megan's diagnosis on March 13, 1998, Patrick was tested and he also had this fatal disease. (Thankfully, John Jr. does not.)

Someone once asked me what a grandfather does when he's told that two of his littlest ones have an incurable disease that will claim their young lives in a matter of months.

I answered as honestly as I could. "First, you cry. Then you get angry."

I held Kathy as she sobbed uncontrollably, knowing there was nothing I could do to lessen her grief in realizing that two of her grandbabies might not live more than a couple more months. And when my wife was all cried out, I took my turn holding my daughter and John and she did the same.

I held them both as they sobbed so hard that neither noticed my tears.

We hugged and we cried until we had no more tears to shed.

And when the crying was done, I got angry.

I mean, really angry.

I mean—and I hope the sisters back in St. John's parish will understand the need for strong talk once in a while—I got good and fucking angry.

Life will serve up tragedy from time to time.

That's just life.

And no one has any control over that.

But what I had learned over the years was that you can control your reaction to those tragedies.

We were, as a unified family, presented with a tragic situation, but we absolutely refused to accept the inherent inevitability of those children's fates. We pulled together and got busy making solutions.

Chapter Forty-Eight

THE SHILL

The difficulty most people have in overcoming problems is that they panic in the face of adversity and abandon the clearheadedness that is necessary to clearly evaluate the situation and then formulate a plan for dealing with it. I'm blessed to not suffer from that handicap.

The first difficulty that we faced was that there was no known cure for Pompe disease—there wasn't even any meaningful research being conducted on the condition. Not really.

So the first step toward saving the kids became jump-starting medical research. And that meant raising money. Lots of it.

John was the spearhead behind the Children's Pompe Foundation, a mechanism for us to begin raising money for medical research. All things considered, that first step was easy enough.

Step two, not so much.

The first step toward saving the kids became jump-starting medical research.

The fact of the matter was that none of us had any background or experience in charitable donations, and I can't say that any of us had any sort of a sound understanding of where or how to begin. The only thing that we were certain of was that we needed to do something and we needed to do it right away.

One of the first events we held was a fundraiser at the Beacon Hill Country Club, where

Kathy and I belonged and all of our children were well known amongst the other members. I can't be sure, but I don't think any of us had a firm expectation for the evening in terms of financial contributions. More than anything, I think we were shell-shocked and looking to our friends for a little support.

They did not disappoint.

Moving around as much as we did as a family, one of the admitted drawbacks was the inability to forge the sort of lasting friendships that are available to those who make themselves at home in a community over a period of decades. That leaves you—maybe inescapably—with a very limited sense of obligation attached to those casual friendships you develop between the last move and the next one.

And yet on that evening I stood feeling like Jimmy Stewart at the bell-ringing final scene of *It's a Wonderful Life*, when the various members of the community respond to his moment of need with a very unexpected show of extraordinary generosity.

We attended the event with no real expectations and left that evening with contributions

> **That evening I stood feeling like Jimmy Stewart at the bell-ringing final scene of *It's a Wonderful Life*.**

totaling $83,000. I was then, and remain to this day, overwhelmed by this display of kindness and compassion.

The most important thing, even above and beyond the gift of friendship we received, was that the foundation had money in its coffers to begin the work that was necessary to find a cure for Megan and Patrick.

And we didn't stop there.

If we didn't have a clue about the ins and outs of charitable fund-raising when we started, we were soon experts in the field.

One of the most vivid memories I have of the time is an auction event that we held in New York City. We had all solicited donations to be sold to the highest bidder, and our friends had really come through for us in extraordinary ways. Each item on the block was more special than the next.

And I bid on every one of them.

Or rather, I did my very best to raise the price as high as I could.

In order to "encourage" competitive bidding, some (less than scrupulous) auction houses will utilize the services of a shill, an individual planted among the assembled crowd for the sole purpose of placing bids intended to drive up the price of the item on the block.

Now as the kids' grandfather and one of the organizers of the event, I lacked the sort of under-the-radar anonymity one might hope for in a shill. To the contrary, I admit I was something of a conspicuous presence that night.

That didn't stop me at all.

If there was a diamond bracelet stalling at ten grand, I bid fifteen.

If people seemed hesitant to go above fifteen thousand for a trip to London, I offered seventeen-five.

Whatever was being auctioned, I bid on it.

By the end of the evening, my vigorous efforts had paid off greatly.

That night, when the event was over and all the items had been distributed to their winners, $500,000 had been raised for the foundation.

It was a powerful night.

Kathy and I shared a car ride back to our hotel.

"That was quite an evening," I said.

I patted her hand.

"You had quite a night for yourself." she said.

I smiled.

She did, too. "You know they were all bidding up and up just to save you from having to buy everything you bid on?"

"That was the plan." I offered her my foxy grin.

"And do you have any idea what it would've cost us if we didn't have such great friends?"

"I do not."

"Seventy thousand dollars."

"Then we're lucky we have such good friends."

"Yes. Yes, we are." She put her head on my shoulder. "But I wouldn't have said no to that bracelet."

Chapter Forty-Nine

THE IRISHMAN AND
THE REBBE

This entire period of my life was overwhelming in so many ways, but certainly my emotions were stretched and strained past limits I thought I'd never survive. And still, it was also an incredible time of learning about the nature of life and the character of the individuals we share it with.

I had a dear friend, Les Turchin, who owned a significant electronics retail chain in New Jersey. I think of him fondly now, but I did not feel that way when we first met.

No, that's not quite right. To be more accurate, I did not like the way he comported himself.

The first time we met, I had flown to New Jersey to meet him at his corporate offices. I was shown to a waiting area just outside his office. I took a seat and tried to overlook the fact that I don't like to be kept waiting.

While I was sitting there, consciously making the effort not to check my watch for the thousandth time, a low rumble on the other side of the office door very quickly grew into a screaming string of obscenities.

After what must've seemed like a lifetime to the poor guy on the receiving end of the verbal beat-down, the door opened and out slunk a young man who looked like he'd been locked in a pillory.

He was followed out by my host, who greeted me with a big smile and a handshake.

All my life I've known bullies. I've known their victims, too. And I've learned that some people have been subjected to so much casual cruelty over their lives that they come to the misguided conclusion that the only way to protect themselves is to become the biggest bully on the block.

I guessed that was the case here.

I was also certain that I wasn't interested in finding out.

As soon as the door closed behind us, I told him, "If you ever speak to me the way you spoke to that young man or I hear you talk to anyone like that again, we're done. Got it?"

Not only did he get it, he seemed to appreciate the gesture.

Or at least he respected it.

From that point on there was never a problem between us, and I like to think that our business relationship evolved over time into a real friendship.

Despite the nature of our relationship, I was still somewhat surprised to receive a call from him one evening.

"Marty," he said. "I have a favor to ask of you."

At the time, I had my hands full with our own issues. We needed to raise more than a million dollars to fund research for the kids, and our chances of doing so seemed less than certain.

Still, I couldn't deny my help to someone who'd come asking. "What can I do for you?"

"I heard about your situation," he said.

I silently shook my head and smiled. I should've known. He wasn't asking for a favor, he was offering one.

"I want you to do me a favor," he said. "Whatever you need, I want you to write it down on a piece of paper and send it to me. I'll take it with me to the Rebbe."

I was touched by the sentiment behind the gesture, but didn't understand exactly what he was offering. "What is that?"

He laughed. "I should've known I'd have to explain it to an Irishman."

I laughed, too.

"Menachem Mendel Schneerson was a great man, an Orthodox rabbi who became known simply as the Rebbe. Over time a tradition grew up in which the faithful would write the Rebbe with requests for his intercession in bringing their requests directly to God. That tradition continued even after he died—people bring their requests to the Ohel where he is buried, and leave it for him there. I want you to send me your letter, and I'll personally bring it to the Ohel and give it to the Rebbe."

I was not just raised Roman Catholic, I was raised Irish Roman Catholic. While I believe passionately in the right of every person to worship (or not) as they choose, I had never considered participation in any religious tradition beyond my own.

And yet I was incredibly touched by my friend's offer.

I sat at my desk and wrote out what I needed to save my grandchildren. Seeing those needs set out in ink had an unexpected chilling effect on me. And if I had ever dared to let myself consider the staggering impossibility of the task in front of us, that might very well have been the moment.

I sent the letter anyway.

A lot of people were involved in the effort to raise money to fund the research we needed to save the kids. There were countless charitable contributions made and a lot of hard business decisions that factored into our reaching that unreachable number. The practical engineer in me knows that.

As a man of faith, I know with equal certainty that there is far more to this world than can be answered or explained with science and cynicism.

And yet as a man of faith, I know with equal certainty that there is far more to this world than can be answered or explained with science and cynicism. "There are more things in heaven and earth ... than are dreamt of in your philosophy," as Shakespeare once wrote.

A year after I wrote the letter and my friend placed it with the Rebbe at the Ohel, we not only met our impossible goal but far exceeded it. In just over two years we had raised three and a half million dollars to fund the medical research of the Children's Pompe Foundation.

We had not only done the impossible, we had exceeded it.

And I believed.

I believed in the kindness and support of friends.

And in the power of prayer, whether that's an Irishman on his knees in a church pew or his Jewish friend delivering a plaintive request on his behalf to the grave of a revered man of faith.

I believed.

And I still do.

I believe not only in a Higher Power that transcends denominational boundaries and encompasses all in a loving embrace, but also in the infinite capacity of people to come together in marvelous and unexpected ways that can transform this world.

Chapter Fifty

A HAPPY ENDING

Kathy and I, and the whole family, continued our efforts to raise the money necessary to fund the medical research needed to find a cure for Pompe disease, but the real story of that struggle lies with Aileen and John and the kids, all of whom routinely displayed courage and character throughout the ordeal that exceeded what I otherwise would have considered the limits of the human heart and soul.

The story of what they endured individually is their story and more insightfully told in John's memoir, *Chasing Miracles: The Crowley Family Journey of Strength, Hope, and Joy,* which he coauthored with Ken Kurson, and more movingly told in the book *The Cure* by Geeta Anand. Geeta's book became the basis of the major motion picture *Extraordinary Measures* starring Harrison Ford, in which John was portrayed by Brendan Fraser and Aileen by Keri Russell.

Still, I am far too proud of their heroic efforts not to offer my own version of events.

After the diagnosis, Aileen and John moved the family back to New Jersey so that they could be closer to family and closer to doctors who were more directly involved in the treatment of the disease. While Aileen stayed with the children, caring for them 24/7, John secured a position at Bristol-Myers Squibb, which gave him the proximity necessary to do his own research into the disease.

This research afforded him an introduction to William Canfield, one of the few medical researchers to work on finding a cure for Pompe, and together they founded a biotechnology research company, Novazyme Pharmaceuticals, for the purpose of obtaining the key to the Pompe cure.

The work Novazyme was involved in was so promising that within a year they were acquired by Genzyme Corporation, which was then the world's third largest biotechnology company. That happened because John was able to put a business face on this rare disease, and Genzyme saw a multibillion dollar opportunity going forward. John was made a senior vice president in charge of the company's Pompe research, and with the limitless resources of Genzyme behind them, there was a drug developed within a year.

There was only one catch. Because John was a senior VP of the company, ethics policies prohibited his children from being a part of the trials.

Because John was a senior VP of the company, ethics policies prohibited his children from being a part of the trials.

How can I describe the painful irony of the decision? We had all worked so hard, accomplished the impossible so that a cure might be developed, and it was John's position at the forefront of the fight that was going to deny those kids the one hope there was to save their lives.

This was not a result John was willing to live with. In order to ensure that his children would be able to participate in the drug trials, John resigned from the company.

And the outcome was more than worth the sacrifice. Enrolled in the trials for the test drug, both Megan and Patrick responded positively. Their hearts, which were swelling as a result of the condition and struggling to continue functioning, began to return to normal size.

Even now, after all of the years have passed, I cannot find the words to express our thoughts and emotions upon learning of the results of those tests. We had come together as a family to face the impossible, never conceding to what everyone else had tried to convince us was inevitable. And yet it was the achievement of that seemingly unreachable goal that packed the most emotional punch.

None of us had really allowed any of the others to consider the possibility that we might come up short, but there was something in their salvation that brought home the reality of just how close we had come to losing our Megan and Patrick. It was an overwhelming tsunami of emotion for all of us.

And I'm pleased and proud to say that the benefits of our efforts now extend far past the Crowley/Holleran contingent. As a result of John's work, the fundraising we all participated in, and the support of so many of our friends, Pompe is no longer the death sentence without pardon that it was when the kids were first diagnosed.

Pompe is no longer the death sentence without pardon that it was when the kids were first diagnosed.

Lives have been changed.

And, more important still, lives have been saved.

John went on to found a second biotechnology company focused on developing next-generation treatments and cures for devastating, rare diseases. He continues to run that company, as Chairman and CEO of Amicus Therapeutics, which has grown into a multibillion dollar company worldwide. Amicus has made significant inroads into the cure and treatment of a number of previously under-studied genetic diseases, including Pompe.

Aileen continues to amaze me—and everyone else in her life— every single day. She has not only cared tirelessly for her children, but extended her concern to others who have had to confront the devastation of a Pompe diagnosis. In part because of her efforts to assist others seeking treatment for their children, Aileen was awarded an honorary doctorate degree from Neumann University. She was also named the "Inspiring Woman of the Year" by the Make-a-Wish Foundation of New Jersey.

Patrick and Megan make every day a miracle for all of us who love them so. Their survival is an inspiration to so many who deal with adversity in their lives. Megan is currently a junior at the University of Notre Dame and writes a blog, *High Heeled Wheels,* which lends her optimistic and humorous outlook to meaningful discussions of the challenges of living with physical disabilities.

And most of all, the family is stronger than ever.

We have a family tradition of celebrating every Christmas Eve at John and Aileen's home. All the kids and the grandkids gather round, and I sit in the middle of them all and read *'Twas the Night Before Christmas.*

As soon as I've begun reading, Marty, my son, surreptitiously disappears from the group and makes his way upstairs, where there's a surprise waiting—a small toy elf, tethered to a fishing line.

And just as I'm reaching the conclusion of the kids' favorite Christmas poem, that elf appears like magic in the window behind my chair. The kids squeal and laugh (even those who are old enough to know it's just Uncle Marty).

Those are the moments that make this life worth living.

Family and friends. Little things like children's laughter and silly toy elves. These are the things that matter.

These are the things that give us the strength to make it through the nights.

And always will.

Chapter Fifty-One

THERE BUT FOR THE GRACE

While we were dealing with one of the most obscure diseases known to man, none of us had even the slightest idea that one of us was dealing with one of the most common.

My youngest son, Brian, married his college sweetheart, Kim, and started a family. He got a job and climbed the ranks until one day he got an opportunity to run a company. The American Dream.

All of us were very proud of him, even if we had all overlooked the toll that his high-pressure life had begun to take on him.

With his professional responsibilities, Brian would put in a full work day, come home to spend time with his wife and kids, and then retire to his home office in the company of a couple of inches of paperwork.

And a bottle of wine.

Every night.

Night after night.

After a while, the stress, the schedule, and that nightly bottle of wine began to get the better of him. He started feeling "a little out of it" and soon ran straight downhill until he was feeling "like hell."

He went to the doctor—I don't think expecting anything more than a prescription for vitamins—and was shocked to learn that he had a liver condition that diminished his body's capacity to process even a normal amount of alcohol. As a result of his hardworking lifestyle, his liver had begun to fail him.

In an alarmingly short time, my youngest son went from feeling rundown to being incapable of dragging himself out of bed. He was unable to work. He was unable to be the father and husband he'd always been. His very life seemed to be slipping away from him.

It turns out there's a numerical measurement for that: MELD.

> **In an alarmingly short time, my youngest son went from feeling rundown to being incapable of dragging himself out of bed.**

The acronym seems innocent enough, but the devastating nature is uncovered in the full name: Model for End-Stage Liver Disease. The number is a metric to measure how close the patient is to death.

Knowing that such a grim figure is applicable to your youngest child cuts you to your core. And in my reaction, I found myself facing a familiar foe—that feeling of hopelessness that initially accompanies such tragic news.

It only lasted a moment or two.

And then I got really angry. Again.

> **I found myself facing a familiar foe—that feeling of hopelessness that initially accompanies such tragic news. It only lasted a moment or two.**

Initially, Brian's MELD score ranged between ten and eleven. For a point of reference, it takes a score of fourteen before the patient is placed on a transplant list. Relatively speaking, it seemed like the situation was somewhat manageable.

And then things turned very suddenly for the worse. Almost overnight, Brian's moderate MELD scores shot up to a range between forty and forty-five, a score that not only shot him to the head of the transplant lists at his hospital in New Jersey, but also carried with it a shattering prognosis of three months life expectancy.

We prayed for a transplant to come through in time—Brian's only hope for surviving.

Then, during one of the numerous exams Brian had to undergo as part of the transplant process, one of the physicians asked if he had taken a drink of alcohol at any time in the previous year.

Brian, queasy from all the medication, answered in the affirmative. Several months earlier, before his condition had even been fully diagnosed, he'd had a couple sips from a glass of wine. That was all.

It seemed a minor admission.

Disclosing those few sips, however, was enough to trigger hospital policy safeguards that immediately removed him from any consideration for a transplant.

It was a death sentence.

And now I got really fucking angry. Again.

But by that I mean that I got proactive. Everyone in the family did, especially my son Marty, who was the real quarterback for his brother at this most critical time of his life.

It turned out that Marty knew a physician in New York who was a liver specialist. It wasn't easy—we weren't worried about easy—but somehow it got done. Within a matter of days, we had Brian transferred from New Jersey to NYU Langone Medical Center and placed on their transplant list.

As we were walking through the final procedures for transferring Brian from the hospital in New Jersey that had issued their "no exceptions" ruling that effectively condemned him to death, one of the physicians who had made that decision approached me. "How in the world were you able to make this happen?"

I understand the importance of policies and the unpleasant obligations that come with positions of leadership. I do.

> **What did you think I was going to do, let my son die just because you said he should?**

And that may be the only reason I was able to restrain myself. "You gave my son a death sentence. What did you think I was going to do, let my son die just because you said he should?"

The doctor didn't have a response.

I think that was for the best. For both of us.

When we finally got Brian settled into his room and confirmed that he was on the hospital's transplant list, we all breathed a collective sigh of relief.

We should've known better.

The hospital reported that while Brian's medical insurance covered the costs of the procedure being performed in New Jersey, the insurer would not extend coverage over the Hudson River into New York.

Without that coverage, the lifesaving procedure that had been pushed past administrative roadblocks now became a financial impossibility.

I'm not sure what infuriated me more: the prospect that my youngest child might die because of an administrative policy or the possibility that he would perish simply because there was not enough money to keep him alive.

Of course, I only stayed angry for a moment or two.

With all of the experience my son-in-law, John, had with insurance companies in handling his own children's claims, he had made a number of friends in the insurance industry. With a call or two (and a favor or two) we had confirmation that the insurance company would agree to cover the procedures for Brian.

If there was any doubt about what was going to happen in Brian's case, I had called my old friend, Larry Johnston—of "laser air conditioner" fame—and asked for his assistance. Larry had risen to the head of the appliance division at GE, but then he left to take the head spot at the Albertsons chain of supermarkets. Along the way to corporate superstardom he'd become friends with some senior officials at NYU Medical Center.

Suddenly, there was no longer a financial issue. Or any issue at all.

With a few telephone calls, my son's life had been saved.

Brian received the transplant and recovered completely.

Today he speaks on the unseen dangers of drinking and other motivational topics.

I'm immensely proud of him.

And I'm even more grateful just to have him with us all.

The experience—knowing that Brian was just days from death—put a different perspective on all of our lives, and I'm grateful for that, too.

Still, there is never an occasion when I hug my son, or answer his phone call with a bit of fatherly advice, that I don't think to myself of all the fathers who faced similar situations but whose stories reached tragic conclusions.

I learned a long time ago about the importance of treating politics as a personal matter best confined to private conversations, and I have no intention of ignoring that important guideline now.

Life, however, shouldn't be a political issue. Health and relief from suffering and offering people the medical assistance they need shouldn't be something that lies beyond the reach of any of us.

Health and relief from suffering and offering people the medical assistance they need shouldn't be something that lies beyond the reach of any of us.

And until that becomes the case in our country, my heart bleeds for those who are disadvantaged in that system.

Chapter Fifty-Two

UNCLE MART

For some people, family is a word that begins with a small "f." Themselves. Their spouse. Their kids. Maybe their parents, or a sibling or two. On a stretch, a real close cousin.

For me, family not only begins with a big "F," but I spell it with all capitals. Maybe it's my Irish heritage, but when I talk about my FAMILY, I'm talking about the entire clan.

Kathy and the kids, grandkids, and my brothers of course.

Cousins and first cousins and second cousins once-removed.

Nieces and nephews.

In-laws and outlaws.

Friends of my family and family of my friends.

Everyone.

My family is my greatest blessing, and I have always tried to nurture them—each and every one of them—and to share with them all of the other blessings that this life has bestowed upon me.

This has earned me a title that I value right up there with husband and father and grandad: Uncle Mart.

I am Uncle Mart to all my nieces and nephews, from the Holleran side and the Jordan side, with equal amounts of love in my heart for them both. And I've always tried to do right by all of them.

I remember one particular night when Kathy and I had only been married about three or four years. We were making the best of the Syracuse winters, and toddler Marty was doting on baby Aileen. Everything seemed so perfect that perhaps we were lulled into a certain suburban complacency.

That's not a complaint. I thoroughly enjoyed every minute of that domestic bliss, in which I was able to maybe forget some of the grimmer life lessons I'd been taught—or at least in which their sting didn't seem so sharp in those days.

And then the phone rang.

Not one of those I-wonder-who-this-could-be calls.

No, this came too late for something that innocuous.

This was one of those calls that shatters the night's silence.

This was one of those calls when you know something has gone very, very wrong and the only question is "What?"

Or "Who?"

I was no stranger to losing people I loved. My mother's passing was still an open wound in my heart and soul.

And I had told others that they had lost loved ones—so often, in fact, that if I listened too hard to the quiet in a sleepless night I could still hear the cries and the wailing.

What I had never done before was tell someone I loved that they had lost someone they loved.

I took the call, listened to the news, and then returned the phone to the cradle.

And then I turned around and caught Kathy's curious gaze. She knew straight away that the call hadn't been for me.

I tried to keep my straight face, my "good soldier" composure, but it was unbearable to watch the eyes that have always been my source of comfort suddenly widen with the excruciating pain that I already knew too well.

All she could ask was "Who?"

Her brother, Joe Jordan, was a helluva guy. In fact, if you needed a picture to stick in the dictionary next to the definition of "helluva guy," his would be a more fitting candidate for that spot than just about anyone else I can think of.

> It was unbearable to watch the eyes that have always been my source of comfort suddenly widen with the excruciating pain that I already knew too well.

Salt of the earth. Great family man. Hard worker. Helluva guy.

It was an accident. That was the thing of it. There was no reason you could attribute to it. No explanation. Nothing to blame.

Just the sort of wrong-place-wrong-time, spin-of-Fortune's-wheel shit that should make every reasonable mortal grateful for each single day.

His loss was an unspeakable tragedy for Kathy.

And his widow, Mary Lou, of course.

But the survivor I was most concerned might not survive the void that death left was his young son Joe, and his three brothers and sisters.

I always made a point of spending extra time with the kid, who now had to face this world without a man by his side. I promised him, "Anything you ever need, you just ask me."

And I meant it.

Joe was a fantastic kid. His dad would've been proud of him, because he grew up to be a helluva guy just like his old man.

One day after graduating from college, he came to me and asked, "Uncle Mart, I really want to go into manufacturing management. Is there anything you can do for me at GE?"

The next day I went to the head of the department and had a word with him.

> I always made a point of spending extra time with the kid, who now had to face this world without a man by his side. I promised him, "Anything you ever need, you just ask me."

The guy said, "Marty, I'd love to help you out but your nephew doesn't have an engineering degree, and that's a no-starter in our department."

I nodded and left him with a "See what you can do."

The next day I was back, and it was the same bullshit story.

On day three, I told the guy, "I'm only going to ask you one more time."

I'm not sure what he read into my comment, but the next day, Joe had an interview with HR about a slot in the manufacturing management program.

Next thing I know, I get a call from that department head. He says, "Marty, we had your nephew down for an interview for our program."

I sat back in my chair. "How'd it go?"

"How'd it go? I told you, no engineering degree, no go. The kid walks into my office, sits down, and I tell him the same damn thing."

I braced for the bad news.

But there was more to the story. "The kid looks me right in the eye and tells me that he appreciates me taking the time to talk to him, but if our program is that shortsighted that they can't look past a diploma to see the true measure of a candidate, then he doesn't think he wants to a part of that kind of program."

"What'd you do?"

The guy laughed. "What could I do? I hired the kid on the spot. He starts Monday."

Joe was the superstar of his program class. He flourished at GE and went on to become the head of manufacturing operations at Gulfstream.

Sometime later, at one of our family get-togethers, he took me aside and said, "Uncle Mart, when my dad died, there were lots of people who came up to me and said that they'd do anything for me. I never saw most of them again. You were the only one who actually did it."

And Joe wasn't the only one of my nieces and nephews that I went to bat for at GE, at a time when I knew that others in positions similar to mine wouldn't have stuck their necks out so far for even their closest relatives.

I mean, don't misunderstand me—I was fortunate enough to have held a place in the company at that time which carried with it a good deal of autonomy and authority. If I wanted someone hired, it was a damn-near certainty that I could've found a place for them somewhere within the company. But I was by no means alone at that level.

The rub, as they say, was that this privilege did not come without a corresponding degree of risk. It was an equal certainty that if my hire screwed up, the accountability would rest not with them, but with me.

And it's for this reason that while there were more than a few of my colleagues at GE who had similar (or far greater) pull, there were very few (if any) who were willing to put their careers on the pass line and take a roll of the dice on anyone but themselves.

And I can't say I blame them. A career is … well, it's a heavy thing to stake for someone else.

But I never had a doubt. Not about any of my own children or the nephews and nieces who found a home (or at least a start) with GE.

Let me make that clear, too.

What I was able to do for my nephews and nieces, that wasn't nepotism.

Nepotism is when you hire someone solely because they're family. That kind of routine always struck a wrong chord with me. When I secured positions for my family, I wasn't doing them a favor as much as I was securing employees for GE who I knew would far exceed whoever else might have been available for that position. These kids were top-notch, sharp, and motivated.

I got my nephew, Eddie Janeski, a spot when I was the top guy at the facility in Englewood Cliffs, New Jersey. On days when one of my kids had requisitioned my car for this "good reason" or that, Eddie would swing by and pick me up to go to work together.

Now, I'm no snob. Never have been—and I figure it's too late to start now. But at the time, Eddie was driving what can only be described as a piece of crap on wheels—and even they weren't aligned.

I remember on one occasion we were on our way to work in his Crap de Ville and the snow was coming down so hard that pretty soon the only thing I could see through the windshield was white.

I thought it would've been obvious, but I turned to him and said, "Eddie, don't you think you should turn on the wipers?"

He looked puzzled. "I would, Uncle Mart, but they don't work."

So there we are pulling into the company parking lot, and the big boss man is leaning out of the passenger window, wiping away the snow with the arm of my coat.

The employees might have laughed at that sight, but I'm still smiling to think of it.

Tommy Ruddy, just like Joe Jordan, lost his dad when he was too young. And just like Joe, it was my privilege to look out for a boy who was challenged early and grew up to be just a fine, fine man.

They excelled, every one of them.

And the fact that I loved them all only made their success all the sweeter.

Chapter Fifty-Three

AIN'T IT AWFUL

From my childhood days in Scranton's South Side to the corporate corner suites, throughout my career and personal life, I have certainly faced my share of obstacles and endured a generous portion of adversity. I'd like to think that I always rose to the challenge, but I know there are occasions I may have fallen short of the bar I set for myself.

Still, the one thing that I have never done is felt sorry for myself.

I firmly believe that if there is one factor that makes the difference between a successful career and a failed one, or between a happy life and a miserable one, it is simply that: the addictive and debilitating practice of self-pity.

> I firmly believe that if there is one factor that makes the difference between a successful career and a failed one, or between a happy life and a miserable one, it is simply that: the addictive and debilitating practice of self-pity.

And if I'm asked, I would answer that this is one of the most pressing problems facing the generations that are just now coming into their own.

I have always made of point of knowing the people my children know, keeping up to date on their friends. Given the number of times that we moved, I've always considered it essential that I be aware of who was becoming an influence in their lives.

And, more than that, I've always enjoyed the opportunity to interact with my kids and their friends. Even though we were almost always the newest family on the block, the Holleran house was always that place where all the kids came to hang out. And while I tried to pass on my worldly wisdom whenever it was asked for, I also enjoyed the opportunity to stay in touch with what was happening with the generations that were following my own.

There's a spirit and curiosity, an openness to new ideas and a passionate commitment in young people that makes for adventurous and engaging conversations. And I've had the great benefit of talking with some of the brightest young people.

One afternoon, John and Aileen had some of their friends over to our house, and we were having a conversation when one of the young men who was going through the business program at Rutgers University said in what I thought was the most offhand way, "Mr. Holleran, you should really come speak at our school."

I thanked him for the compliment, but was surprised (and extremely honored) when I received a call from the business school's dean inviting me to be that year's commencement speaker.

Glossophobia, the fear of public speaking, is the most common phobia; over 25 percent of Americans suffer from it. I am not one of them.

I thank my mother and her insistence on all of those singing and dancing lessons, but I have always felt at home on a stage.

But while I knew I would be fine in delivering my address, I was less certain about what I should make the subject of my speech.

I've sat through a lot of commencement speeches, and far too many of them were forgettable. Not because of any deficiency in the speaker, but because it's all too easy to overlook the purpose of such talks. It shouldn't merely be a perfunctory exercise to offset the receipt of a honorary degree. It should mean something. It should be something that actually serves the graduate, prepares them for the road they're just about to embark upon.

That was a tall order.

I scribbled out a half-dozen drafts, but none of them met my criteria. I read other speeches and browsed through books of quotes. I considered what the Jesuits had taught me and tried to distill what I'd learned over the course of three decades in corporate America. And I considered the one thing I would want to tell my own children if I was limited to just twenty minutes or so.

And what I came up with was this: ain't it awful!

I've heard that over and over again, all my life. And it's not that I'm unsympathetic to the twist of fates that befall us all—quite the opposite—but all too often that sad refrain and the outlook that gives it voice mutate from an expression of genuine and temporary exasperation to a more permanent excuse to refrain from taking responsibility or action.

All too often that sad refrain and the outlook that gives it voice mutate from an expression of genuine and temporary exasperation to a more permanent excuse to refrain from taking responsibility or action.

Sadly, I think this is particularly common among some younger people whose parents, impacted by childhood struggles not unlike my own, went out of their way (and maybe too far) to make their children's lives as "perfect" as possible.

The efforts are, no doubt, well intended, but the results are all too often disastrous, with young men and women who are unable to face up to life's challenges without falling back down again and moaning, "Ain't it awful!" You know I would have done better in that class but for that teacher! "Ain't it awful!"

That was it.

That was the message I wanted to share with the class graduating from Rutgers' business school.

And with whomever else might do me the favor of considering my words.

Life is hard. That's a given.

There are no exceptions.

None.

And so, since those occasional hardships absolutely cannot be avoided (forget for a moment the consideration of whether or not they should be avoided), the only choice any of us have lies solely with how we respond to such situations.

And even then, there are really only two options.

The first. The easiest. The most common response is to back away from the challenge, to cower at the dangers contained. And I understand this. It is human nature to avoid perceived pain and to seek comfort instead, and I would not be completely honest if I were to insist that I have always resisted this avenue.

Nevertheless, life has taught me that, without exception, this is always the wrong response.

And wallowing in self-pity will never accomplish anything but to worsen the situation and limit the possible solutions to it.

The other alternative is to simply acknowledge whatever misfortune has occurred— "Ain't it awful!"

And then assess the situation to find the opportunities it contains. (Here's a hint: no matter how bleak the situation may appear, there are always opportunities hidden amongst the darkest shadows. Our family's fight with Pompe disease led to significant advancements in its treatment. My youngest son's near-death situation brought about a reborn Brian who has improved the lives of countless individuals with his motivational speeches. There is ALWAYS an opportunity.)

> No matter how bleak the situation may appear, there are always opportunities hidden amongst the darkest shadows.

And then the last step is to simply work.

The temptation is to curl up in a ball and pull the covers up. That will only lead to more problems—and bed sores.

Adversity needs to be fought actively. Often this requires more than anyone could reasonably expect of themselves. But if that's what it requires, then that's what must be done.

And in the end, that's all that really matters. The discomfort and fear are only temporary states, as is the strain of working harder than previously thought possible.

The rewards, however, last a lifetime.

Ain't it awful?

Maybe. But with a little faith and a lot of hard work, it will not only be all right. It'll be great.

When I was done with my address, I received applause, as any speaker expects, but the reception was even greater than I could have hoped for. Not in the obligatory hands, but in the reaction of my audience.

It was clear to me that I had made the connection I'd hoped for with many of the young men and women in that audience.

And even today I like to think that when one of them stumbles or runs straight into some seemingly insurmountable obstacle, they remember the words of the well-intentioned old man who spoke at their business school commencement and think to themselves, "Ain't it awful? Yeah, it is. But I can do it!"

Chapter Fifty-Four

PROTÉGÉS

George Lee Anderson is unquestionably one of the greatest figures in professional baseball. Ever.

He was signed as an amateur free agent to play shortstop for the Brooklyn Dodgers, but he never made it to "the bigs." Not a single at-bat. In fact, his longest stay in pro ball was with the Toronto Maple Leafs. (No, not the legendary hockey franchise, but a Triple-A farm club in the International League.)

So, how can I say that this man, who never played in the major leagues, is one of baseball's greatest figures?

Because the Maple Leafs (baseball, not hockey) were owned by Jack Kent Cooke. (Yes, *that* Jack Kent Cooke. Football. And basketball.) And after watching a series of practices, Mr. Cooke realized that while maybe Anderson's glove and bat were never going to get him any further than Toronto, the guy had an undeniable way with teaching the game to the team's rookies and bringing the best out in the others on the team. Cooke suggested that his sparky shortstop should take up managing instead.

The rest, as they say, is history.

In 1970, Anderson was signed to his first big-league managerial post with the Cincinnati Reds and greeted with headlines across the hometown sports page that read "Sparky Who?"

It wasn't long before the entire country had the answer to that one. Sparky Anderson was the engineer of the Big Red Machine, which reigned as a dynasty that will always be mentioned in heated barroom debates over "the greatest of all time."

Pete Rose. Johnny Bench. Joe Morgan. Tony Perez. Dave Concepcion. George Foster. All of them baseball immortals.

None of them would have reached the heights they hit without Sparky's mentoring and development or without being a part of the team that he assembled, coached, and drove to greatness.

And when his time ran out in Cincinnati, Sparky went up Highway 75 and did the same thing for the Tigers, developing yet another roster of untapped potential into World Series champions.

> **Sparky Anderson, a man who found greatness in finding the greatness in others.**

Sparky Anderson, a man who found greatness in finding the greatness in others.

Although I think I made my way to the show and put up career numbers that stand on their own, I've always respected Sparky Anderson and others like him, because, truth be told, I have always found greater satisfaction in being part of a team and fostering others than I've derived from my own private and personal successes. And that was the way that I always went about my career, particularly in my supervisorial and managerial role.

I remember I once had a guy in a marketing department I oversaw.

Nice person. Terrible marketing guy.

I gave him advice.

And encouragement.

And constructive criticism. None of it worked. In fact, it only made him worse.

Now, I am by nature and personal choice a generally happy guy. I would always rather share a laugh and a smile and put my best effort into making the business "dance."

> I have always found greater satisfaction in being part of a team and fostering others than I've derived from my own private and personal successes.

Still, Jack Welch … and the U.S. Army before him … and the Jesuits before them … and the parish nuns before them, had all taught me that there comes a point and time in life when nothing else will do but to put boot to ass.

And this kid's time came up with me.

I started with some not-so-gentle criticism, but the blank look with which he received it somehow suggested to me that he still wasn't grasping the seriousness of the situation—or the grimness of his future. So I let him have it.

Really have it.

Jackie Gleason. "One of these days … Boom! Pow! To the moon!"

When I was done, the kid looked like he'd gone thirteen rounds with Ali. He slunk out of my office and spent the remainder of his day slumped at his desk.

I felt no better for it either.

At the end of the day, I asked the kid to go have a couple of beers with me. Over a couple of frosty ones, we talked it all out. Straighten up. Do better. No hard feelings. Go in peace.

The next week came … and the guy did worse. I would've sworn that was an impossibility, but this guy would've proven me wrong. It was a tough situation, because the next stop for the kid was a one-way trip to Pink Slip City, and I've always hated handling that duty.

More than that, however, I couldn't help feeling that as much as he was screwing up his job, I had failed him as a mentor and supervisor in providing him with whatever guidance or incentive he needed to do his damn job.

I called him back into my office. He had that gallows look to him.

I said, "When I chewed you out last week, you went home and told the wife, right?"

He hung his head a little lower. "Yes."

"You told her what an SOB your boss is and how he rode your ass for no reason, right?"

His head dropped again. "Yes."

"Well, buddy," I said. "I thought you were lousy as a marketing man, but you're even worse as a husband."

His eyes grew wide and he looked up at me. (It was the first real sign of life I'd seen from him in months.)

"You go home and tell your wife how mean the boss is, but you didn't tell her about going out for beers and clearing it up, did you?"

"No."

"Well, you just did your wife the biggest disservice. She thinks the love of her life is getting picked on and she gives you all kinds of sympathy, because that's what you want. But what she needs to know is that you're going to take care of things."

He nodded. "Yes, sir."

"And that's what I need, too. I need to know that you're going to take care of things. You're not going to sit around feeling sorry for yourself, you're going to pull yourself together and take care of things. I want you to go back to your desk and instead of feeling sorry for yourself because the boss yelled at you again, I want you to be grateful that you still have a boss—because I have to tell you that's looking like less and less of a certainty. And when you go home to your wife, I want you to tell her that today was a great day—because you've got a job and a paycheck and that makes every day a great day—even the shitty ones."

He got up and shook my hand. "Yes, sir. Thank you, sir."

Now, I'm not going to claim that he came in the very next day as a new man, but he did return as an improved one. And that improvement continued, little by little, day by day, until one day he was actually doing his job.

Better than that, he was good at his job. Very good.

I'd moved on to another opportunity and another position before I got to see the full conclusion of that story, but I'd like to think that his improvement continued and his situation, both in the office and at home, was improved because of our intersection.

And whatever success he earned through his new attitude and his own hard work, I'd like to think that there was a small part of it that he attributed to the boss that chewed him out so badly.

And bought him a beer or two.

And I'd like to think it's that way with a lot of people who worked for me over the years, and a few that I worked for, too.

Of course, I'll never know. One of the drawbacks to the gypsy nature of my career was that there was always a new challenge, a new facility, and a new set of coworkers. But I'd like to think that despite the miles that eventually came between us, that every one of them knows how much they meant to me as teammates. And friends.

While too many of my former protégés have realized their success without my further involvement in their lives and careers, there have been a few whose meteoric ascendancies have made it quite easy to keep an eye on them.

I met Jimmy Meyer when he was just a young finance guy with RCA, right after the GE takeover. From the very first conversation I had with Jim I knew that he was my kind of person.

And I knew he was a winner in every way.

In my desire to maintain a balance between RCA vets and my new guys from GE, I made Jimmy my finance guy, but the truth is that he would've been my choice no matter what blend I'd been looking to achieve.

It's funny, because he didn't accept my offer right away. He thought the position was significantly above his level of experience—and I can't say that he was wrong.

"I don't know, Marty," he said. "I don't know that I can do the job."

"Do you want the job?" I asked.

He nodded.

"Then take the job. And find a way to get it done."

And that's exactly what he did. In our time together, he distinguished himself over and over again not only as a genius with figures (and he was), but as a guy who understood that the most important factor behind the balance sheet was the flesh-and-blood people who were represented in all of those numbers. He was a funny guy, with a sharp wit and always ready to make his point (even if that was a shot across the bow) with a smile and a joke.

I moved him from finance to running the Canadian sales operation for Thomson, because I knew he needed the experience— and that he would flourish in it.

And flourish is exactly what he did. After a distinguished career at Thomson, he went on to become president of Aegis Ventures. That led to a position as president, operations and sales, for SiriusXM Radio.

Today he's SiriusXM's CEO.

Of course, as amazing as Jimmy's success has been, he's not the only protégé who rose to levels of celebrity status.

I've already told the story of how Larry Johnston brought sexy back to window air conditioning units with our laser exhibit at the Las Vegas trade show.

And, of course, after that flashy debut, he went on to enjoy a long and distinguished career at GE.

Beyond GE, he went on to become the Chairman/CEO of the Albertsons supermarket chain, one of the largest food and drug retailers in the world. Ever the forward thinker, Larry revolutionized the marketplace and brought a number of cutting-edge innovations to the Albertsons stores which are now commonplace and ubiquitous throughout the retail world.

But I've also told you the part that Larry played in our efforts to save the life of my youngest son, Brian, and so more than anything else, I will always remember Larry for that role that he played in my life and the lives of those I love.

I enjoyed every minute I spent in the executive's chair over the course of my career, and I'd like to think that unlike Sparky Anderson's tour of the minors, I spent my time in the majors and put up more than respectable numbers in the big leagues.

But like Sparky, I think that my greatest strength—or at least what I found most satisfying—was bringing out the greatness in those around me. And like Sparky, I'm confident that over the course of my career I put together more than a few teams that deserve to be considered among the best of all time and whose members all benefited from one another.

I was then, am now, and always will be eternally grateful to each and every one of them.

Chapter Fifty-Five

MERRYCK

I (for the most part) enjoy people, and like my father before me, I'm always trying to "crack their face" with a smile. But then, I've always had a gift—given to me and developed by my parents—for what I like to call "people skills," the ability to understand what's important to people and to treat them in a way that conveys the depths of my sincere respect for those interests.

And I think this is the reason why I've always placed team building and mentoring at the very top of my corporate skill set.

But while my talents for interpersonal communication were always one of my strong games, I'd never really found a position where those abilities could be the total focus of my professional efforts.

I was consciously aware of this when the success we achieved with the Children's Pompe Foundation created an opportunity for me to reenter the workaday world and find my next professional challenge. The situation with Megan and Patrick had been so desperate and difficult that I had stepped away from the corporate world (I was running a public company, Projectavision) in order to focus my attentions full time on developing the Foundation with John Crowley to achieve significant financial success and providing the personal support that was needed every bit as badly as monetary investments.

But with the "happy ending" that we received in response to our hard work and prayers came the realization that it was time for me to begin to write another chapter. A new chapter.

I was eager to reenter the corporate world, and it seemed natural—or at least, appropriate—for me to again assume an executive position that would allow me to navigate one enterprise or another through the dire straits of doing business. But at the very same time, there was something deep within me that held reservations about charging *"once more unto the breach, dear friends ..."*

Initially, I did return to corporate America. First, I took a position as CEO of Genca, a subsidiary of General Cable. Then I was brought in to do a major turnaround as CEO for Electrolux Home Care Products.

Both of these were terrific opportunities, and I'm proud of the fact that the success I achieved on behalf of both companies more than exceeded all of the expectations that came with the positions.

But something was still ... missing.

And then—as has so often been the case in my life—something just happened.

This time, that particular happening was a call from a gentleman named David Carter, who was the head of Merryck, a corporate mentoring group that had become very successful throughout the United Kingdom and Europe and that was looking to make headway in the United States.

And what David had to offer was very intriguing to me.

Merryck didn't offer the typical business strategies and solutions that are the traditional fare of consulting groups in the States. Instead, they provided a personal program that walked a CEO or other high-level management executive through a regimen that identified that individual's personal characteristics and then mentored them to address those aspects that needed improvement. Rather than fixing a particular problem, Merryck enabled the executive to solve all of their problems all by themselves, thereby taking their game to the next level.

It was an interesting prospect, but I remained uncertain about where exactly I might fit into their plans.

Dave and I talked back and forth over a period of time, but I was less than convinced—not about the wonderful work that Merryck was doing on behalf of their corporate clientele, but that there was an opportunity there for me to find the position I had been looking for.

In the midst of my searching, David extended a gracious offer for me to visit with him in London, but even after our meeting I remained uncertain about taking those next steps forward.

Before I could make it back to Heathrow for the flight home, however, David asked me for one favor. He had a client, a guy who ran a major European telecom and who had faced some difficulty in finding a suitable match as a mentor. David wondered if I could take an hour or two to talk to the gentleman and at least provide some insight as to what I thought might be appropriate for him to look for in a prospective mentor moving forward.

It seemed a harmless exercise to occupy an evening in London.

David had us both to dinner.

We talked.

And then to my complete surprise, the telecom CEO asked *me* to be his mentor.

Two weeks later, I found myself at a retreat with the gentleman, reviewing the mentoring process ahead of us.

And that's how—completely unexpectedly—I finally found my professional home.

Still, when I came aboard at Merryck, David asked me to be the CEO. I told him that I was only interested in a two-year stint, long enough for his group to get established in the States and to find someone else to assume the position of running the company's day-to-day business. We were able to accomplish this and hired David Reimer, the former CEO of Drake Beam Morin.

We also had the great good fortune to fill our Chairman position with Richard Mills Smith, former editor-in-chief, CEO, and Chairman of *Newsweek*. Over the course of his distinguished journalistic career, Rick had the opportunity to interview every CEO of any significance, and the depth of his business knowledge is really astounding.

Today, Merryck has established itself as the premier CEO mentoring program in the United States. This assertion is in no way a commentary on other services offered to the executive community, but rather to highlight the distinction between the respective services offered.

There are plenty of distinguished consultancy groups that offer sound business advice, market analysis, strategic planning, and other similar assistance in the daily operations of a given business. This is not what Merryck does.

Similarly, there are armies of coaches who have studied and been trained in offering performance assessment and coaching with regard to a particular aspect of a business or specific skill sets. This is not what Merryck does.

What sets Merryck apart from really anyone else is that the mentoring offered is not intended to address a particular issue or problem, but rather to holistically assist the executive in becoming stronger not only in their professional capacity, but also as an individual.

To accomplish this, Merryck starts the mentoring process by utilizing the services of former executives who have distinguished themselves in every level of business and who know *everything* that is involved in sitting in the CEO's chair.

> **What sets Merryck apart from really anyone else is that the mentoring offered is not intended to address a particular issue or problem, but rather to holistically assist the executive in becoming stronger not only in their professional capacity, but also as an individual.**

While coaches and consultants can study this aspect or that, until someone has actually operated in that capacity there is simply no way of fully understanding the full load of those demands or the qualities that are necessary in order to meet them.

Merryck is now staffed by twenty-two full-time mentors, all of whom had distinguished careers as CEOs and who are intimately aware of not only those aspects of the job that would be apparent to most anyone (e.g., leadership command, affirmative decision making, etc.), but also those more subtle conditions that would likely escape anyone without firsthand knowledge of the full executive experience (e.g., personal loneliness, weight of responsibility, etc.) This unique position of servicing an executive with other executives enables Merryck to offer them services that are customized to each and every individual client.

As a metaphor, a coach is like buying a high-end suit off of the rack.

A consultant is like buying a high-end suit off of the rack and then having it tailored.

Merryck is a bespoke suit.

Confidentiality is essential to the mentoring process and fiercely protected. Merryck does not release the results of any of the underlying testing, conversations with mentors, or subsequent status updates with anyone other than the client. No exceptions. Ever.

The retreat at the beginning of the mentoring process may well be one of my favorite parts of the process, because invariably the mentee will say to me, "Marty, I like you and all, but what the hell are we supposed to talk about for two damn days?" As I write this, I've mentored fourteen CEOs and I've yet to have a client who hasn't utilized all of that time—and asked for the opportunity to extend our conversation. Following the retreat, we meet face-to-face monthly and have phone conversations in between.

I think that's why the process works so well—because until most people have the opportunity to become a part of it, it's impossible to realize just how important the service can be in every aspect of their lives. The official mentoring continues for several years, but unofficially lasts much longer.

I'm also fairly sure that's why I find it so rewarding to play a part in it.

I've received a lot of honors and accolades over the course of my career, but I don't think any of them were more important to me than the compliment paid to me by one of my mentees, Brian O'Malley, CEO of Domino Foods. Brian said, "Marty's driving mission was to help me succeed. Trusting him gave me the confidence to work through a variety of issues with a very capable and seasoned professional whose only concern was me. The best analogy I can think of is the relationship between a professional golfer and his caddie. Except in this case the caddie was a former champion and had played the game at the highest level."

Words like that mean everything to me.

And they make me think back to that dark night when I stood by the fax machine with my letter of resignation in my hand. I wish I'd had the opportunity to pick up the phone and talk to a mentor about my situation and the potential solutions to it. In fact, as I look over my career, one of the few regrets that I have is that while I had the good fortune to work with many individuals who impacted and shaped my life to some degree, I never found the one individual I could truly consider as a mentor.

That's not a complaint, just an observation.

And I know only too well that I was not alone in that situation.

Corporate executives are only now beginning to emerge from a sort of emotional dark ages that my peers and I experienced in our careers, a time in which we were all expected to bear the enormous weight of leadership without ever displaying any of the emotional indicators related to those burdens. No one was ever supposed to see us sweat, and asking for help of any kind was all too often seen not as the expression of strength that it really is, but as a symptom of some perceived weakness.

> Corporate executives are only now beginning to emerge from a sort of emotional dark ages.

As a result, far too many individuals struggled with their respective situations, and an equal number of enterprises found themselves without a leadership that was in optimal condition for executing those all-too-important responsibilities. It was an unnecessary lose-lose proposition for all involved.

Today, the growing awareness of the importance of a well-balanced life and developing emotional intelligence have made Merryck a recognized necessity for optimal executive performance and something of a status symbol on par with a home in a certain neighborhood or membership in an exclusive club.

And the future looks brighter still.

Chapter Fifty-Six

CODE OF THE ROAD

I've received any number of honors and awards over the course of my career. Each and every one of them was received gratefully and humbly. But I don't think there are many that have meant more to me than being named one of the Top 100 Irish-American Businessmen.

As I may have mentioned, growing up in Scranton's South Side was not unlike being raised in a county in Ireland itself. (The Hollerans come from Connemara.) And throughout my life, that Irish ancestry has played a significant role.

In addition to the singing and dancing lessons, I'd like to think that my parents gave me the "gift o' gab," and this has served me as well, if not better, than any other skill I have mastered—or ever possibly could have.

I have held any number of positions across the spectrum of corporate divisions: engineering, manufacturing, quality control, marketing, and sales. I have held top positions in several companies.

I have played a role in raising millions of dollars. And the most important tool I used in each and every one of those positions was simply my interpersonal skills. The ability to tell a joke. And listen. To "read" people. To connect with those around me.

Those were the skills that I used most often in building my career. And the tools that I rely on even to this day in my work with Merryck.

> **The most important tool I used in each and every one of those positions was simply my interpersonal skills. The ability to tell a joke. And listen. To "read" people. To connect with those around me.**

With all of the importance that is now placed on business school as a necessary precursor to a corporate career, it strikes me as strange that they don't teach those skills. They really should.

They'd be doing their students a great service.

And the business world as well.

As I said, I'd like to think that whatever talents I have in that department come to me through my Irish ancestry, but they were no doubt honed in my formative years by my brothers.

We've lost Jack tragically, but the three of us are as close now as we were as boys growing up on top of one another in that tiny house on Prospect Avenue. Over the years, my brothers have been my most trusted confidants and the fiercest of allies.

Charlie is still as mischievous as he was as a Catholic schoolboy, but I haven't made many major decisions in my adult life without running them past him first.

Jimmy, the baby of us, enjoyed the designation of being the cool uncle to all of his nieces and nephews, a tradition that continues now that they're grandnieces and nephews. He's the erudite Manhattanite among us, and as each of the kids reached "those years," Uncle Jimmy would always arrange for a special weekend to show them the city—and give them their first glimpse of the real world.

Over time the three of us have developed a tradition—every few years we have a golf trip to Ireland. We see the sights and sing the old songs. We share stories we'd thought we'd forgotten and laugh and bask in the warmth of family—those who are there with us in the flesh and those who are constant companions in the memories we hold in our hearts.

We have a Guinness or two and we raise our glasses to our ancestors, the stalwart ones who survived the oppression and the hardships, the brave ones who faced unimaginable odds to make a life in a new world.

We toast our mother, gone too soon. And our father, who's with her now and always.

And Jack, always our big brother.

Our wives, our children, and our grandchildren. All of those wonderful components of our lives that mean so much more than a boys' dream ever could (Dad was right).

But we save the last toast for one another. The Holleran boys. Together till the end.

Chapter Fifty-Seven

THE REAL ME

While I know I could never minimize the seriousness of those tragedies that I have had to contend with from time to time throughout my life, I have always been aware—even in the darkest depths of those trying days—that on the whole, I have been so much more fortunate than a guy from Scranton's South Side ever had reason to believe I might be.

Over the course of my career, I have been privileged to hold a string of positions that challenged me intellectually and rewarded me with the company of so many fantastic people that it would be impossible for me to make individual mention of them all and criminal of me to fail to call out any one individual. Each and every one them were and continue to be my dear, dear friends.

And while the nuns of my Catholic school days always had a ruler at the ready for any braggadocios kid who might have forgotten their lessons of humility, I'm confident that my knuckles would be safe from one of their scolding attacks if I were to say that in addition to the treasured friends I've amassed, my career has always had an ascendant trajectory that has brought me ever-increasing rewards in terms of responsibilities, prestige, and other more worldly rewards.

I am aware that there are many people for whom these hard-won accomplishments might serve as self-defining achievements, but they never were for me.

I have always been proud of and grateful for whatever nameplate happened to be hung on my office door, whether that was merely "Manager" or "President and Chief Executive Officer."

None of them, however, was ever a description of who I was.

For me, that definition of self was always to be found in family.

For me, that definition of self was always to be found in family.

I am one of the four Holleran boys: Jack, Marty, Charlie, and Jim. I have never been prouder to have been a part of any group, gang, or club than I am to have stood shoulder-to-shoulder with these guys.

I am the most fortunate father in the world. No exceptions. I remember challenging my children when they were growing up, letting them know that they had been given privileges I never could have dreamt of at their ages, but that their situations were so much more challenging than mine because it was incumbent on them to take what their parents had given them and build on that foundation to create something greater (in every sense of the word) still.

Marty, Aileen, and Brian have each not only risen to that challenge, but far exceeded whatever loving expectations (hopes and dreams, really) that Kathy and I ever could have held for them. They are, each of them in their own ways, so much better human beings than I am, and

I am unspeakably proud of the myriad of ways in which they eclipse their old man.

I am a grandfather. Seven times over.

There are many differences between being a parent and being a grandparent, but I think that one of the greatest lies in the fact that no matter how much you might have read or tried to prepare for being a parent, you can never really know what is coming your way with parenthood.

When Kathy and I welcomed Marty into the world, I held my newborn son and knew absolutely that I was going to do everything in my power to love, protect, and foster him to become the man that even then I had every confidence he would become.

But that's about all I knew for sure when it came to parenting.

By the time Kathy and I had raised our kids to a point where they were having kids of their own, however, we pretty much knew exactly what to expect from the process, all of the joys and all of the heartaches, too.

I'm not sure what is better. Knowing or not knowing.

What I can say for certain, however, is that my grandchildren have brought me an unparalleled sense of fulfillment, a warm realization that I have completed my part in some unwritten bargain with ancestors of ancient pasts. I have raised my children, and now they too have carried those traditions on to future generations. They have taken the baton I passed to run races of their own.

And what incredible kids my grandchildren are!

For all the greatest of reasons, much has been written and said about Megan and Patrick and their courageous fight to overcome Pompe disease and the endless challenges that it has brought to their lives. Every day for them is an Olympic accomplishment that I could never fully imagine, and their heroism inspires me constantly to meet whatever obstacles (mere speed bumps in comparison) that I might face in any given day.

What sometimes gets lost in the telling of that story, however, is their older brother, John Jr. He was just a child himself—and facing his own struggles—when he learned that both his little sister and his little brother were so sick that they might not always be with him. And while any eldest child necessarily struggles with losing parental attention to younger siblings, John found himself in a family that was necessarily heavily focused on his brother and sister—which is in no way to say that he didn't always get all the attention he needed from both his mother and father.

I am simply saying that some other kid might have used that particularly difficult experience as a selfish excuse to act out, but John handled it like a champ.

In the midst of our family tragedy, I had the great fortune of spending a considerable amount of time with John, and I was always impressed by his infinite capacity for speaking his mind.

There has never been any sugarcoating with John. None.

Even as a young boy, he called them exactly like he saw them and expected me to do the same. And that's just how we regarded one another and continue to do so to this day. We have always extended to one another the courtesy of unfettered frankness and absolute honesty, and that is why I will always count him amongst the best of my friends.

Our Brian and Kim have four children. Three strapping young men: Connor, captain of his high school football team and now at Rutgers University; Jack, also captain of his high school football team and attending community college; and Ronan, who is in eighth grade and a star player in Pop Warner Football. And each of them is kept in check by their sister Bridget, who is captain of her high school cheerleading squad.

Father. Grandfather. I have cherished each and every one of these roles, but none of them would have ever been possible if I hadn't been, first and foremost, the man who was lucky enough (by some celestial intervention I've never been foolish enough to question) to win the heart of Kathy Jordan all of those years ago.

My *Anam Cara.*

Together we have formed a partnership that made every single one of my personal accomplishments possible and blessed me with a personal life that has given meaning to my life—and definition to me, as a man.

I have had the enormous pleasure and privilege of holding many titles, but in my heart I have always been and will always be, simply, Kathy's Marty.

Chapter Fifty-Eight

SMILE

I learned a long time ago that there's really only one way to judge a person.

It's not by the accolades they've garnered or the wealth they've accumulated.

It's not the fame they've attracted or even the place they may have etched for themselves in the ever-changing annals of history.

The most accurate way to judge a person is to simply say their name, mention them to someone who knows them ... and then wait for the reaction.

> **The most accurate way to judge a person is to simply say their name, mention them to someone who knows them ... and then wait for the reaction.**

It's not whatever praise that follows or the measured words of diplomacy that matter, it's the very first reaction that counts. If the very first thing a person does when they hear a name is smile, then there is no more accurate indicator that this person was one of the good ones.

A *mensch.*

Duine onóra.

A helluva guy.

I have made more mistakes than I could ever count, and I'm grateful for most of them.

The regrets I have are really only a handful or so, and I can live with the ones I've got.

I have endured tragedies that I was certain would shatter my soul and shared joys that were so overwhelming I still cannot contain all that love that fills my heart.

But, all in all—and maybe most important of all—my life has been well lived.

And so all that I can hope for is that whenever you hear my name … I hope you smile.

About the Author

Marty Holleran holds over thirty years of corporate executive experience and has led multinational companies and fast-growth startups through IPOs and turnarounds. Marty held senior executive and CEO roles in companies such as GE, Thomson Consumer Electronics Sales and Marketing Company, Emerson Radio, Projectavision, InnovAlarm, Electrolux Home Care Products NA, and Genca. While working at GE, Marty was selected to participate in the Presidential Executive Interchange Program in Washington D.C. where he held a key government leadership role as deputy administrator at the department of agriculture. Throughout his extensive career, Marty has served on the Board of Regents at Catholic University, on the board of directors at St. Josephs College, and as a board chairman of GFR Consulting. Alongside his son-in-law, Marty also founded the Children's Pompe Foundation which funded the research to find a cure for the rare disease. Mary has received the Torch of Liberty Award from the Anti-Defamation League and was named to the Irish Business 100 Top Executives. Marty is currently vice chairman and executive mentor of Merryck & Co. Americas and a member of its board of directors. He has mentored CEO's, C-suite executives, and senior leaders in the telecommunications, food manufacturing, construction, engineering, pharmaceutical, biotech, and energy industries. He and his wife Kathy have three children and seven grandchildren.

For more from Marty, please contact
MARTY.HOLLERAN@MERRYCK.COM

Aileen and John Crowley

Marty with Ronan and Kathy

Holleran Grand Children:
Connor, Ronan, Bridget
and Jack

Kathy with Jack and Marty

Aileen, Kathy, and John at Notre Dame

Marty and Ronan

Marty with sons
Marty and Brian

Ronan in Marty's office

Marty, Kathy, and Megan at
her high school graduation

Brian, Aileen and Marty

Kathy and Marty with the grandkids

Aileen and Kathy

Marty and Kathy

Jim, Charles, and Marty at
1522 Prospect Avenue

Patrick Crowley

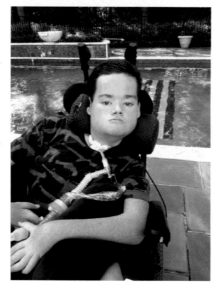

Bridget and Kathy

*Marty with Nipper and
Chipper*

Kathy and her sisters
AnnMarie and Mary

Aileen and Kathy

Marty, Jim, and Charles in
Ireland in 1988

Marty with Megan and Bridget

Marty Holleran

Marty and Kathy's wedding party in 1965

*The Holleran and
Crowley Family*

Brian and Marty

Jim, Marty, and Charles

*Holleran Family: Jack, Dad,
Charles, Mom, Jim,
and Marty*

Marty, Uncle James and Jack

John Crowley Jr.

Kathy and Marty in Paris in 1991

MARTY HOLLERAN

Jim, Marty, and their father
in Ireland in 1981

Larry Johnston, Marty,
and Brian O'Malley

Marty's parents on their
wedding day in 1940